Pope Clement XIV

Interesting Letters of Pope Clement XIV.

Vol. II

Pope Clement XIV

Interesting Letters of Pope Clement XIV.
Vol. II

ISBN/EAN: 9783744675246

Printed in Europe, USA, Canada, Australia, Japan

Cover: Foto ©Lupo / pixelio.de

More available books at **www.hansebooks.com**

INTERESTING
LETTERS
OF POPE
CLEMENT XIV.
(GANGANELLI.)

TO WHICH ARE PREFIXED,

ANECDOTES OF HIS LIFE.

TRANSLATED FROM THE FRENCH EDITION PUB-
LISHED AT PARIS BY LOTTIN, JUN.

VOL. II.

LONDON:
Printed for T. BECKET, Corner of the Adelphi, Strand.
M DCC LXXVII.

LETTERS, &c.

LETTER LXXXII.

TO PRINCE SAN-SEVERO.

THE petrefactions I have sent you are not worth your thanks. I know the full value, as well as the advantage, of entering into a correspondence with a Philosopher who is occupied in studying the history of Nature, and who does not admire her sports and phenomena, but with a knowledge of the cause.

The birds you are importing from the New World for the Emperor, are extremely curious; but, notwithstanding every precaution, I doubt of their getting to our climate alive. People have frequently tried to bring over different kinds of humming-birds, but always have had the

the mortification of seeing them die at some distance from our coasts.

Providence, in giving us the Peacock, has provided us most richly, without our going in search of winged beauties elsewhere. In reality, America has nothing more beautiful than our own birds; but we commonly prefer what is foreign, because it comes from a distance.

You will be enchanted, my Lord, with the undertaking of Monsf. Buffon, the French Academician, and with the volumes which have appeared. I know them only by the extracts that have been given from them, and they appear admirable. I am sorry that the Author of a Natural History should declare for a system: it must be a means of having many things which he advances doubted, and oblige him to combat all those who are not of his opinion. Besides, wherever he wanders from the book of Genesis on the creation of the world, he has no support but paradoxes, or, at best, hypotheses.

Moses, as an inspired Author, is the only one who could instruct us in the formation

mation and unfolding of the world. He is not an Epicurus, who has recourse to atoms; a Lucretius, who believes matter to be eternal; a Spinosa, who admits a material God; a Descartes, who prates about the laws of motion; but a legiflator, who announces to all men without hefitation, without fear of being mistaken, how the world was created. Nothing can be more fimple or more fublime than his opening: *In the beginning God created the Heaven and the Earth.* He could not speak more assuredly, if he had been a spectator;- and by these words, mythology, fyftems, and abfurdities fhrink to nought, and are mere chimeras in the eyes of reafon.

Whoever does not perceive the truth in the relation of Mofes, was not formed for the knowledge of it. Some people are conftantly attached to hypothefes, without even the leaft probability, and yet are unwilling to believe what gives the higheft idea of the power and wifdom of God.

An eternal world offers a thoufand greater difficulties, than an eternal intelligence; and a co-eternal world is an abfurdity which cannot

cannot exist, because nothing can be so ancient as God himself. Not to mention that he is necessary, and that the world is not necessary; from what right shall matter, a thing quite contingent, absolutely inert, pretend to the same prerogatives with an all-powerful and immaterial spirit? These are extravagances which could only be produced by a distracted imagination, and prove the astonishing weakness of man when he will only hearken to himself.

The history of Nature is a book shut for all generations, if we do not perceive the existence of God, and his being a creator and preserver; for nothing can be more evident than his action. The Sun, all magnificent as he is, although adored by different nations, has neither intelligence nor discernment; and if his course is so regular as never to be even for a moment interrupted, it is through the impulse received from a supreme agent, whose orders he executes with the greatest punctuality.

Wherever we cast our eyes over the vast extent of the universe, we see the immensity ty of a Being, before whom this world is as nothing. It would be very extraordinary, since the smallest work cannot exist without a maker, that this world could have the privilege of owing its existence and its beauty to itself alone. Reason digs frightful precipices for itself, when it hearkens only to the passions and senses : and reason without faith is to be pitied. All the Academies of the universe may fancy systems, on the creation of the world; but after all their researches, all their conjectures, all their combinations, their multitudes of volumes, they will tell me much less than Moses has told me in a single page; and will tell me things, too, that have not any probability. Such is the difference between the man who speaks only from himself, and the man who is inspired.

The Eternal smiles from on high at all these mad systems, which fancifully arrange the world; sometimes giving chance for its parent, and sometimes supposing it to be eternal.

Some people love to persuade themselves that matter governs itself, and that there is no other deity; becaufe they well know that matter is ftupid and inactive, and therefore need not dread its effects; while the juftice of a God, who fees every thing, and weighs every thing, is dreadful to the finner.

Nothing can be more beautiful than the hiftory of Nature, when it is united to that of Religion. Nature is nothing without God; it produces every thing, vivifies every thing by his help. Without being any part of what compofes the univerfe, he is the movement, the fap, and the life of it. Let his activity ceafe, there will be no more movement in the elements, no more vegetation in plants, no more fpring in fecond caufes, no more revolutions of the ftars. Eternal darknefs muft take place of light, and the univerfe become its own grave.

The fame thing would happen to this world, were God Almighty to withdraw his hand, which happens to our bodies when all motion ceafes. They fall into duft, they are exhaled in fmoke, and it is not even known that they ever had exifted.

If

If I had sufficient knowledge to undertake a history of Nature, I would begin my work by displaying the immense perfections of its Author; then treat of man as his master-piece; and succeffively from substance to substance, from kind to kind, I would descend to the smallest ant, and shew in the smallest insect, as well as in the most perfect angel, the same wisdom shining forth, and the same almighty hand employed.

A picture of this nature must have engaged the lovers of Truth;—and Religion herself, who would have traced out the design, would have rendered it infinitely precious.

Let us never speak of the creatures, except to bring us nearer to our Creator: they are the reverberation of his never-failing light, and these are ideas which either raise or debase us; for man is never more diminutive nor more grand, than when he considers himself in his relation to God. He then perceives an Infinite Being whose image he is, and before whom he is but as an atom: two apparent contradictions, which must be reconciled, to give us a just idea of ourselves,

selves, that we may not run into the excesses of the proud angels, nor into those of unbelievers, who level themselves with the beasts that perish.

Your Letter, my Lord, led me to these reflections; and I confess to you at the same time, that I have no greater satisfaction than when I find an opportunity of speaking of the Deity. He is the element of our hearts, and it is only in his love that the soul blossoms.

Happily, I was sensible of this great truth in my earliest years, and in consequence I chose the Cloister, as a retreat where, separated from the creatures, I could commune more easily with the Creator. The commerce of the world is so turbulent, that while we are in it we scarcely know the recollection necessary to unite us with God.

I thought of writing a Letter, and I have wrote a Sermon; except that, instead of finishing with *Amen*, I conclude with the respect which is due to you, and with which I have the honour to be, &c.

ROME, 13 December, 1754.

LETTER LXXXIII.
TO COUNT ALGAROTTI.

IT is a long time, my dear Count, since I have had the pleasure of conversing with you, or rather, since I was at your school. A little disciple of Scotus cannot do better than profit by the lessons of a Philosopher, who has brought to light the Newtonism of the Ladies.

A philosophy on the subject of attraction ought more particularly to be yours, because you have such an attracting, amiable character, that you draw all minds after you; but for my part, I would rather, with such advantages, be less a Newtonian, and more a Christian.

We were not created to be either the disciples of Aristotle or Newton. Our souls have a much nobler destiny; and the more yours is sublime, the more you ought to remount to its source.

You may say as often as you please, that it is the business of a Monk to preach; and I will repeat to you continually, that it is the business of a Philosopher to employ himself in thinking from whence he came,

came, and whither he goes. We have all a cause, and final purpose for our existence, and it must be God alone who is both the one and the other.

Your philosophy, notwithstanding your reasonings, rests only upon chimeras, if you separate it from religion. Christianity is the substance of the truths which man ought to seek after: but he loves to nurse himself in error, as the reptiles love to satiate themselves on the mud in the ditch. We seek at a distance what we may find in ourselves, would we only look within, as did the great St. Augustine; who having taken a view of every being, to see if he could find his God, returned to his own heart, and declared that he existed more there than any where else—*Et redii ad me.*

I hope you will preach to me one day, and that each of us shall have his turn. Ah! I wish to God!—However, whether you moralise or banter, I will always hear you with that pleasure which one must have in hearing those they cordially love, and to whom they are from inclination as well as duty, the most humble, &c.

Rome, 7 December, 1754.

LETTER

LETTER LXXXIV.

TO THE ABBE PAPI.

BEHOLD, my dear Abbé, the learned Cardinal Quirini is juft gone to unite his knowledge to God, and to take full draughts from that torrent of light, which we cannot perceive here below, but through clouds. He died as he lived, with his pen in his hand, finifhing a line, and ready to go to Church, where his heart always was. Mine fhall erect a monument to him within myfelf, as lafting as my life. He had a regard for me—but, alas! for whom had he not? His cathedral, his diocefe, all Italy, even Berlin, has experienced his liberalities. The King of Pruffia honoured him with fingular efteem, and all the Learned of Europe admired his zeal and his talents.

He had a conciliating turn of mind;— all the Proteftants loved him, though he often told them fevere truths. It is to be regretted that he did not leave fome confiderable work, inftead of writing only detached pieces. He would have encreafed the Benedictine

nedictine Library, already so voluminous; and being one of the moſt diſtinguiſhed members of the Order of St. Benedict, he would have enriched the Church with his productions.

If Poets are ſuſceptible of friendſhips, Monſ. Voltaire will regret him. They correſponded amicably;—genius ſought after genius. For me, who can only admire great men, and regret the loſs of them, I ſhall ſhed tears upon the tomb of our illuſtrious Cardinal. *Quando inveniemus parem?*

I have the honour to be, &c.

CONVENT OF THE HOLY APOSTLES,
13 January, 1755.

LETTER LXXXV.

TO A PAINTER.

WHILE there is expreſſion in your pictures, my dear Sir, you may applaud yourſelf for your work. That is the eſſence of the art, and renders a number of faults excuſable, which would not be forgiven in an ordinary Painter.

I have

I have spoken of your talents to his Eminence Cardinal Porto-Carrero, and according to your defire, he will recommend you in Spain; but nothing will make you better known than your own genius;—one muſt be born a Painter, as well as a Poet. Carrache, notwithſtanding the ſpirit of his pencil, would have produced no work worthy of attention, if he had not poſſeſſed that rapture which inſpires with enthuſiaſm and ardour.

We ſee in his pictures a ſoul which ſpeaks, which animates and inſpirits: we think we can become Carrache himſelf, from the ſtrength of admiration, and be filled with the juſtneſs of his images.

How the ſpirit of that great man, whom you have choſen for a model, breathes in you! You will revive him again upon the canvas! If you were only his ſhadow, you would deſerve to be eſteemed : the ſhadow of a great man has ſome reality.

Nature ought always to be the model for every man who paints; and to execute it well, no efforts are neceſſary. Painters, like Poets, become monſtrous, when they

they strain their genius in composing. When talents are in a proper disposition for executing a work, a man feels himself hurried on by an irresistible propensity to seize the pen or the pencil, and give himself up to his inclination, without which he has neither expression nor taste.

Rome is undoubtedly the true school to form a Painter; but whatever trouble he takes, he will never rise above mediocrity, unless he has genius.

It is time for me to have done, since a Counsellor of the Holy Office is not a Painter, and we have every thing to lose, when we speak of what we know only imperfectly.

I am, Sir, &c.

LETTER LXXXVI.

TO MONSIGNOR AYMALDI.

YOU have reason to be surprised, my Lord, at the happy alliance which is henceforth to unite the houses of Bourbon and Austria. There are prodigies in politics

.tics as well as in nature; and Benedict XIV. on learning this surprising news, had reason for exclaiming, O *admirabile commercium!*

M. de Bernis has immortalised himself by this political phenomenon, having had juster views than Cardinal Richlieu.

By this means we shall have no more wars in Europe, except when they grow tired of having peace; and the King of Prussia, though always thirsting after glory, will not seek to make conquests. But I see Poland at his mercy; and because a hero equally valiant and fortunate loves to aggrandize himself, he will one day take part of it, if that part be only the town of Dantzick. Poland itself may perhaps lend a helping hand to such a revolution, by not watching sufficiently at home, and splitting into a thousand different factions. The patriotic spirit is no longer sufficient among the Polanders, to animate them to defend their country at the expence of their lives. They are too often from home, to retain their national spirit. It is only in England that the spirit of patriotism is never extinguished, because it is founded on principle.

Europe

Europe has always had some warlike Monarch, jealous of extending his territories, or gathering laurels: sometimes a Gustavus, sometimes a Sobieski, sometimes a Louis the Great, sometimes a Frederic. Arms more than talents have aggrandised empires, because mankind have known that there is nothing of such energy as the law of the strongest, the *ultima ratio regum*.

Happily, we feel none of these calamities here: all is in peace, and every one relishes its fruits deliciously; as I eminently taste the pleasure of assuring you of all my esteem, and all my attachment.

LETTER LXXXVII.

TO THE ABBE NICOLINI.

Sir,

I Was extremely sorry that I was not at the Convent of the Holy Apostles, when you came to favour me with a visit before your departure. Alas! I was upon the banks of the Tiber, which the ancient Romans magnified as they did their triumphs;

nymphs; for as to its length or breadth, it is but an ordinary river.

This is a walk which I have a particular liking to, from the ideas it infpires me with on the grandeur and declenfion of the Romans. I call to mind the times when thefe fierce defpots held the world in chains, and when Rome had as many Gods, as they had vices and paffions.

I then fhrink back into my cell, where I employ myfelf about Chriftian Rome, and where, though the loweft in the houfe of God, I labour for its utility: but it is a work which is prefcribed, and therefore tedious; for in ftudying, a man commonly loves what he performs freely.

I dare not fpeak to you of the death of our common friend; — That would be to tear open a too tender wound. I came too late to hear his laft words. He is regretted like one of thofe fingular men of whom his age was not worthy, and who poffeffed all the candour of the primitive times.

It is faid that he has left fome pieces of poetry worthy of the greateft mafters. He never mentioned them, which is the more

extra-

extraordinary, as Poets are seldom more discreet with regard to their writings, than to their merit in other respects.

For some time we have had a swarm of young Frenchmen here, and you may believe that I have seen them with much pleasure. My apartment was not large enough to hold them; they all did me the favour to come and see me, because they had been told that there was a Monk in the Convent of the Holy Apostles who had a particular love for France, and every one that came from thence. They all spoke together, and it was an earthquake that gave me much pleasure.

They do not like Italy too much, because it is not yet quite frenchified; but I comforted them, by assuring them that in time they would complete the metamorphosis, and that I was already more than half a Frenchman.

I have the honour to be, &c.

ROME, 24 July, 1756.

LETTER

LETTER LXXXVIII.

TO MR. STUART, A SCOTCH GENTLEMAN.

IF you are not affected by the fluctuation of the waves which surround you, I will reproach you keenly for your inconstancy; for inattention to an old friend, who has been constantly attached to you, is not to be forgiven. Your conduct reminds me of what I have often thought, that the principal nations of Europe resembled the elements.

The Italian, according to this similitude, represents the fire, which, always in action, flames and sparkles; the German, the earth, which, notwithstanding its density, produces good pulse and excellent fruits; the French, the air, whose subtlety leaves not a trace behind; the English, the fickle wave, which changes every instant.

A skilful Minister, with address, chains these elements as he finds necessary, or makes them wrestle one against the other, according to the interests of his master. It is what we have seen more than once when

Europe was in combuſtion, and was agitated by reciprocal violences.

Human policy embroils or reconciles according to intereſt, having nothing more at heart than to govern or aggrandiſe. Chriſtian policy, on the contrary, does not know the criminal art of ſowing diviſions; but its greateſt ſucceſs is in preventing them. I cannot value policy which is not founded on equity, for that is Machiaveliſm put into action: but I have the moſt advantageous idea of a policy which is ſometimes quiet, ſometimes active; is governed by prudence; meditates, calculates, foreſees, and after having recalled the paſt reflects upon the preſent, glances into futurity, and having all times in view, becomes active, or remains inactive.

It is abſolutely neceſſary that a good Politician ſhould know hiſtory perfectly, and the age in which he lives; he ſhould know the degree of ſtrength and ſpirit poſſeſſed by thoſe Characters, who appear on the ſtage of the world; to intimidate them if they are weak, to oppoſe them if they have courage, and to miſlead them if they are raſh.

A know-

A knowledge of men rather than of books, is the science of a good Politician, and it is of consequence in his affairs to know those perfectly whom he is to employ. Some are only proper for speaking, while others have courage which fits them for action; and all depends upon not mistaking their characters. Many politicians fail from having misplaced their confidence. There is no recovering a secret when it has once escaped, and it is better to commit a fault by being too reserved, than by an imprudent confidence: *What we do not speak, cannot be wrote.*

The fear of being betrayed renders him pusillanimous, who has too lightly laid open his heart. There are circumstances where the Politician should appear to say every thing, though he says nothing; and be able to mislead with address, without betraying the truth; for it is never lawful to change it.

It is not weakness to yield when we cannot do otherwise; it is then wisdom. All depends on knowing the proper moment, and the characters of those you have to deal with;

with; to foresee certainly the effect which resistance could have in such circumstances.

Vanity often proves very hurtful to a Politician. When impelled by resentment, we would triumph over our enemy, and are easily entangled in difficulties, from not foreseeing the consequences.

He who would lead men, ought to subdue his passions, and oppose a cool head to those who have the greatest warmth; it is that which makes us commonly say, *that the world is the inheritance of the phlegmatic.*

The way to disconcert the most impetuous adversary, is by great moderation.

We should have much less quarrelling and fewer wars, were we only to calculate what quarrelling and fighting must cost. It is not sufficient to have men and money at our disposal; we must know how to employ them, and reflect that fortune is not always in the hands of the strongest. For a long time we have had nothing but a temporising policy at Rome, because we are weak, and the course of events is the happiest resource to extricate those who cannot resist. But as this is now a secret of which no one is ignorant, and as our flowness in determining is generally known, it is not amifs, but even proper, for a Pope now and then to be determined; not in things that may be difputed, but in things that are juft; without which the Sovereign Pontiffs would be of certain being oppreffed every time they are threatened.

Unfortunately, war is neceffary for fome nations to become opulent; there are others, again, to whom it proves certain ruin: from all which I conclude, that a Minifter who knows how to profit ably of circumftances is truly a treafure; and when a Sovereign has the happinefs to find fuch a man, he fhould preferve him, notwithftanding cabals.

I have been ftammering upon a fubject which you underftand much better than I do; but one word leads on to another, and infenfibly we fpeak of what we do not know.

Thus it happens in letter writing.—We do not forefee all that we fhall fay. The foul, when it comes to recoil upon itfelf, is aftonifhed, and with reafon, at its fertility.

It

It is a striking picture of the production of a world from nothing; for our thoughts, which did not exist a little before, suddenly start into being, and make us sensible that the Creation is really not impossible, as some modern Philosophers pretend. I leave you with yourself; you are much better than with me. Adieu.

ROME, 22 August, 1756.

LETTER LXXXIX.

TO THE REV. FATHER ***, APPOINTED CONFSESOR TO THE DUKE OF ***.

WHAT a charge! What a burden! my dearest friend. Is it for your destruction, or for your salvation, that Providence has appointed you to this formidable employment? That idea ought to make you tremble.

You ask me what you should do to discharge it properly?—Be an Angel.

All things prove shelves and snares for the Confessor of a Sovereign, if he has not patience to wait God's good time, gentleness to compaſſionate imperfections, and ſteadineſs to reſtrain paſſions. You ought to be filled, more than any one, with the gifts of the Holy Ghoſt, ſo as to diffuſe ſometimes hopes, ſometimes fears, and always inſtruction. You ſhould have a zeal capable of ſtanding the ſevereſt teſt, and a ſpirit of juſtice to balance the intereſts of the people, and the Sovereign of whom you have the guidance. You ſhould firſt endeavour to know, whether the Prince whom you direct is inſtructed in the duties of religion, and his obligations towards his ſubjects; for, alas! it is too common for Princes to come out of the hands of thoſe who had the forming of them, without any knowledge but what is ſuperficial. Next you ſhould oblige your penitent to inſtruct himſelf, and to draw inſtruction from their true ſources, not loading the memory with many lectures, but ſtudying by principles what Religion and Politics require from a governor.

There are excellent works upon this ſubject, and you ought not to be ignorant of them. I know one that was compoſed for Victor-

Victor-Amadeus, and which has no other fault but that of being too diffuse, and exacting too much.

When the Duke is solidly instructed, for he should not sleep over frivolous ceremonies, recommend to him to seek truth continually, and to love it without reserve. Truth should be the Sovereign's compass. It will be the means of getting rid of all informers and Courtiers, who support themselves in Courts by flattery and falsehood, and who are by a thousand degrees the most dangerous of all scourges; destroying Princes both for this world and the next.

Insist, without intermission, on the necessity of shewing the respect that is due to religion, not by inspiring a spirit of persecution, but by recommending an evangelical courage, which spares the person, but stops the scandal. Repeat frequently that the life of a Sovereign, like his Crown, is very insecure, if he suffers jesting about the worship due to God, and does not put a stop to irreligion.

Endeavour by your firmness, by your representations, by your prayers, and even by your tears, to make the Prince whom you guide,

guide, diftinguifh himfelf by the goodnefs of his morals, and to caufe them flourifh in his kingdom, as they conftitute the tranquillity of citizens, and the happinefs of families, which is the feed of population.

Reprefent to him frequently, that his fubjects are his children, and that he fhould be a parent to them day and night, to help and comfort them; that he fhould not impofe taxes upon them, but in proportion to their wealth and induftry, fo as neither to expofe them to indigence nor defpair; and that a ready adminiftration of juftice is his indifpenfible duty.

If you do not engage him to fee every thing with his own eyes, you will do your duty only by halves. The people are not made happy but by entering into particulars, and there is no means of knowing them, without defcending to make the enquiry.

Though the Great defpife the people, and do not reflect, that in a State the People comprehends every individual except the Sovereign, yet to you, let that people be ever prefent, as a facred portion with which the

Prince should be constantly engaged;—a portion which makes the support of the throne, and which should be watched like the apple of the eye.

Make him sensible, that the life of a Sovereign is a life of trouble, and that recreations are only permitted to him, as to the rest of mankind, for relaxation; and teach him to know, that he ought to stop his christian studies, and even his prayers, if he is wanted for the support of the state.

Speak to him of the dreadful account which he must render to God of his administration, and not of the judgment which history pronounces against bad Princes after their deaths. That is not a proper motive to actuate a religious Prince; for history is only the voice of men, which perisheth with them: but the living God, the punisher of crimes, is the object which should regulate the conduct of a Sovereign. It is of little consequence to most people, whether they are well or ill spoken of after their death; but the sight of an eternal and inflexible Judge makes the most aweful impression upon the human mind.

You

You will not prescribe those vague penances which consist in simple prayers, but apply a remedy fit to heal the wounds which will be exposed to you; and particularly endeavour to discover what is his prevailing fault; without which you may confess for a whole age without knowing your penitent. If you would stop the course of an evil, you must go to the fountain-head.

Take great care not to step beyond the bounds of your ministry, and not meddle, I do not say with any intrigue, but with any business, of the Court. It is most unworthy to see a Monk, who ought not to appear but as a representative of Jesus Chirst, dishonour that august function by sordid interest or detestable ambition.

All your desires, all your views, should have the safety of the Prince who places his confidence in you for their sole object. Astonish him by an incorruptible virtue, always equally supported. If a Confessor does not make himself respectable, and especially in a Court, where they only seek pretences for not being Christians, he authorises thorifes vices, and expofes himfelf to be defpifed.

Inculcate into the mind of the Prince, that he muſt be anſwerable to God for all the employments he beſtows, and all the evil which is done in conſequence of his making an improper choice. Repreſent to him particularly, the danger of nominating ignorant or vicious people to eccleſiaſtical dignities, and nouriſhing their effeminacy and covetouſneſs by giving them a plurality of benefices. Perſuade him to ſeek out merit, and to recompenſe thoſe who write for the good of the public, and for Religion. Teach him to ſupport his dignity, not by pride, but by a magnificence proportioned to the extent of his dominions, his forces, and his revenues; and to deſcend, at the ſame time, from his rank, to humaniſe himſelf with his people, and to ſearch after true happineſs.

Place his duty frequently before his eyes, not with ſeverity nor with importunity, but with that charity, which, being the effuſion of the Holy Spirit, never ſpeaks but with prudence, ſeizes the proper ſeaſon, and profits by it. When a Prince is convinced of

the

the knowledge and piety of his Confeffor, he hears him with good-nature, if his heart be not corrupted.

If your illuftrious pupil accufes himfelf of effential faults in adminiftration, fpeak to him in general terms, and you will come infenfibly to the point of making him confefs what you ought to know. You fhould often infift upon his hearing all his people, and doing them immediate juftice.

If you do not find yourfelf inclined to follow this plan, retire; for thefe are precepts which you cannot tranfgrefs, without rendering yourfelf guilty both in the fight of God and Man.

The function of an ordinary Confeffor does not attract the public attention, but all eyes are fixed on the conduct of the man who is Confeffor to a Sovereign. You cannot be too exact in the tribunal of penitence, in not allowing any one to approach to the facraments whofe fcandalous life muft render him unworthy in the eyes of the public. There are not two Gofpels, one for the Sovereign, and another for the people: both the one and the other will be equally judged.

judged by that unalterable law, becaufe the law of the Lord remaineth eternally.

Princes are not the images of God by their power and authority only, which they hold of him alone; they are fo likewife by the virtues which they fhould poffefs, to be proper reprefentatives of him. A people fhould be able to fay of their Sovereign, " He governs like a Deity, with wifdom, clemency, and equity:" for Sovereigns are accountable to their fubjects for their conduct; not to difclofe the fecrets of the Cabinet, but in doing nothing which can miflead them.

Of all things, take care not to falfify the truth, either from weaknefs or any worldly motive. There is no capitulating with the law of God; it has the fame force at all times, and the fpirit of the Church is always the fame. The zeal of the great Ambrofius with regard to the Emperor Theodofius, is extolled by the Church as highly at prefent as it was formerly; for fhe neither varies in her morals nor opinions.

I pray to God, with all my heart, that he may fupport you, and enlighten you in

fo

so hazardous an employment, where you ought not to be an ordinary man, but a heavenly guide. You will then live as a hermit, in the midst of the great world; as a truly religious man, in a dwelling where there is commonly but little religion; as a Saint, in a place which would destroy the men of God, if the Lord was not every where with his elect.

    I embrace you, and am, &c.

ROME, 26 April, 1755.

LETTER XC.

TO THE PRELATE CERATI.

MY LORD,

AT last the Chapter of Dominicans, at which our Holy Father solemnly presided, is over, and the Rev. Father Boxadors, equally distinguished by his birth and merit, hath been elected Superior General. He will govern with much wisdom and honesty, as an enlightened man who is acquainted with mankind, and knows that they are not to be governed imperiously.

    Benedict

Benedict XIV. who opened the Session with a discourse the most eloquent and flattering for the Order of St. Dominick, which has always been remarkable for the understanding and virtue of its members, desired to have the Rev. Father Richini for General, a truly modest and learned Monk; but notwithstanding his presence, and all his wishes, he could not succeed.

The Pope took it very well, and in going away, smiling, said, " that the Holy " Theresa having asked Our Saviour, where- " fore a Carmelite, whom he had declar- " ed to her should be chosen General, was " not elected, he answered her, *I was for* " *him, but the Monks were against him.* It is " not astonishing then, added our Holy " Father, that the will of his Vicar hath " not had its effect."

All the world knows that we too often resist the Holy Spirit, and that mankind daily defeat the intentions of the Deity by their wicked ways.

Father Bremond is little regretted, although he was extremely affable and virtuous. His Order reproached him with having a blind condefcenfion for a brother who governed him, and whom I always diftrufted, becaufe he appeared to me to be a flatterer. It is feldom that men of that character are not falfe. Your fweetened language is rarely the language of fincerity.

I pitied poor P. Bremond, without daring to blame him. What man in employment but has been deceived?

There are many people unjuft with regard to the Great, and efpecially when they are not great themfelves. The circumftance of the Great being befet with cares and embarraffments is not attended to, which fhould in part excufe them, when they cannot fee all with their own eyes. Happy he who only fees greatnefs at a diftance, like a mountain which he has no inclination to climb!

I have the honour to be, &c.

Rome, 29 July, 1756.

LETTER XCI.

TO AN ENGLISH LORD.

I Cannot conceive, my Lord, inftructed as you are in the imperfections of human nature, the variety of opinions, the fantafticalnefs of tafte, and the force of cuftoms, why you fhould be aftonifhed at the form of our Government. I do not pretend to juftify it, as it neither favours commerce, agriculture, nor population; that is to fay, what is precifely the effence of public felicity: but do you think there are no inconveniences in other countries?

We are under an infenfible Government, it is true, which excites neither emulation nor induftry; but I fee you Englifhmen under the yoke of a populace who drag you as they pleafe, and who, by their impetuofity, which cannot be reftrained, become your Sovereigns: and I fee other people, fuch as the Polanders, under an anarchy, and the Ruffians under defpotifm; without mentioning the Turks, who dare not fpeak for fear of the Sultan, who can do whatever he pleafes.

It

It is generally imagined, though I do not know why, that the Ecclesiastic Government is a sceptre of iron; yet whoever has read its history, cannot be ignorant that the Christian Religion has abolished slavery: that in those countries where it still unhappily prevails, as in Poland and Hungary, the peasants, who are under the government of bishops, are not bondsmen; and that, in fine, nothing is more gentle than the dominion of the Popes. Besides their never having war, being necessarily Princes of Peace, they trouble nobody either for taxes, or their ways of thinking.

There are certain Inquisitions which have caused the Priests to be branded with the name of Persecutors. But, besides that the monarchs who authorized them, were equally guilty with the instigators, Rome was never seen to give in to the barbarous pleasure of burning its citizens for want of the faith, or because some improper discourse had escaped them. Jesus Christ, expiring upon the Cross, far from exterminating those who blasphemed him, sollicited their pardon with his Father: *Pater, ignosce illis.*

What is certain is, that although some ministers of God have sometimes declared for blood and carnage, they have only done it by an enormous abuse of religion, which, having charity for its essence, preaches up meekness and peace.

Yet, wheresoever I look round the world, I see that, in the midst of our indigence and apathy, we are still the people who live most happily. This is owing, it is true, to the goodness of the soil and climate, which furnishes us abundantly with the necessaries of life.

If our Government had more activity, there would certainly be more vigour and circulation in the Ecclesiastical State: but who hath told us that the Government would not then become despotic? The luke-warmness of the Popes, commonly too old to undertake or execute, makes at once both our misfortune and our happiness. They leave the country to produce what it pleases, without attending either to its culture or improvement; but they crush nobody under the weight of taxes, and every one

one is fure of remaining in peace at home, without the leaft moleftation.

Rich countries are taxed in proportion to their riches; and I do not know, in fact, whether it is better to inhabit a country flourifhing by its induftry, and having exorbitant burdens to pay, which leaves only the means of fubfifting; or to live in a place without this circulation, but in a happy eafe. It appears to me that every individual, feparately, loves rather to gain little with nothing to pay, than to gain much, and pay almoft the whole. I prefer having only twenty-five fequins to myfelf, to the happinefs of poffeffing a hundred out of which I muft pay ninety.

We are frequently mifled by fpecious advantages in what we fay upon Government. The whole world requires undoubtedly that we fhould labour and be active, lending our hands to one another from the moft diftant parts of the globe, and by keeping up correfpondences fupport a juft equilibrium, or at leaft a happy harmony: yet that does not hinder but there may be a little corner in the world which

may

may be happy, without taking a part in all these enterprises and revolutions; and we are in that little intrenchment where the serpents of Discord do not hifs, and where Tyranny doth not exercise her cruelties.

The human mind is always in motion, because man is perpetually agitated: he never loves to see countries reft in torpid indolence. Thus conquerors who ravage kingdoms, who plunder, who kill, and usurp, please him much more than those beings who remain fixed in one place, leading an uniform life, and who do not, by their revolutions, present him with any interesting spectacle on the theatre of the world.

Nevertheless, the life celebrated by Philosophers and Poets is not a life of tumult; they banish avarice and ambition from the mind of man to render him happy; and in this they agree with the true Christians, who preach up disinterestedness and humility.

I assure you, I have often estimated every kind of Government, and I should be puzzled to decide which is the best. None of them are without their inconveniences;
and

and at this we should be the less surprised, since the universe itself, though governed by Infinite Wisdom, is subject to the strangest revolutions. Sometimes we are crushed by thunder, sometimes afflicted by calamities, and almost always vexed either by shocks of the elements, or by the plague of insects; in the heavenly country only all will be perfect, and there we shall find neither evils nor dangers.

A little less enthusiasm for your country, Sir, would make you allow that there are abuses in it as in other countries. But how expect an Englishman not to be an enthusiast in favour of his country? You will tell me, that the liberty and property of your citizens are singularly respected with you; and I will answer, that these two prerogatives, which essentially constitute happiness, and which ought never to be invaded, remain equally inviolate in the dominions of the Pope. There every one is allowed to enjoy his property in peace, to go and come as he pleaseth, without being molested. The rigours of authority are unknown in the Ecclesiastical States,

States, and you may say, that the superiors have more the manner of entreating than commanding. Do not imagine, from these observations, that I am an apologist for a government so defective as ours: I know its defects as well as you; but think that there is not an administration in the universe of which we may not speak both good and ill. May the republican love republics, and the subjects of monarchs love monarchies, and then all will be in its proper place. As for me, I am in mine, when I assure you of the respect, &c.

ROME, 27 September, 1756.

LETTER XCII.

TO A PHYSICIAN.

I Am grieved, my dear Friend, that your domestic affairs are still in so bad a situation, and that your wife, by her excessive expences, labours continually to make them worse. There is nothing but patience and mildness which can affect her. Gain her confidence, and you will afterwards gain what you please. You should never molest a wife,

what-

whatever she may have done amiss; but fall upon some means capable of opening her eyes. Speak reason to her; seem to enter into her views so as not to have the appearance of contradicting her; and insensibly, by candid representations, by good treatment, by sensible reasonings, by the effusions of the heart, she may be brought to relish the morals you preach to her; but you must not assume either a pedantic manner, or the tone of a moraliser.

Above all things, do not complain of your wife before your children, but still less before your servants. They will acquire the habit of no longer respecting her; perhaps they may despise her.

Women deserve attention, and the more so, as it is almost always the temper of husbands, or domestic vexations, which make them peevish. Their tender forms require attention, as well as their situation, which does not permit them to divert their cares so easily as we can do, whose lives are divided between business and study. While the husband goes abroad on business or pleasure, the wife remains confined at home,

home, necessarily employed in minute attentions, which are consequently teizing. Women who love reading have a resource, but they cannot be always reading: besides, almost every woman who reads much is vain.

 I advise you to recommend to her creditors, to come frequently to persecute her, when she is in their debt. She will soon grow tired of their visits, and then you should take occasion to shew her, that there cannot be a greater misfortune than to be in debt when we cannot pay. You will engage her attention by mentioning the necessity of saving something for her children. She loves them tenderly, and that motive will be the best lesson which can be given her.

 I formerly knew an old officer at Pesaro, who had suffered much by the passionate freaks of his wife. When she fell into a rage, he remained immoveable, and did not speak one word; and this silence very soon cooled her passion. The passionate are to be disarmed by mildness.

 How pleased am I, my dear Doctor, that I am married to my cell! It is a quiet companion, who does not speak one word, who

does

does not put my patience to the trial, and whom I find always the same at whatever hour I return; always tranquil and ready to receive me. The vexations of the Monks are nothing, when compared with those of people who live in the world; but it is neceſſary that every one ſhould ſuffer patiently, and reflect that this life is not eternal. St. Jerome ſaid, that he adviſed marriage to thoſe only who were fearful in the night, that they might have a companion to keep up their courage; but as he was never fearful, he never inclined to marry.

I am glad that your eldeſt ſon has ſuch an uncommon ſagacity. You muſt work upon the temper of the youngeſt, ſince he is more reſerved, that he may ſhew himſelf. The talent of a father is to multiply himſelf, and to appear to his children under different forms: to one, as a maſter; to another, as a friend.

The confidence which the firſt people of the town place in you does them honour. They muſt have known, from frequent cures, that the reproaches againſt phyſicians are

not

not always well founded. The fashion is to be merry at their expence; but for my part, I am convinced that there is more understanding among them than in almost all the other professions; and that their science is not so conjectural as is commonly thought: but man, ingenious in deluding himself, says, that it is never death, but always the physician that kills. Besides, what learned man never deceives himself? We should not see so many sophisms and paradoxes in books, were it not that writers are fallible, though they know a great deal.

What I say to you, my dear Doctor, is the more generous on my part, because I enjoy the most perfect health, and have no need of any physician. I take my chocolate every morning, lead a frugal life, use a great deal of snuff, and walk frequently; and with such a regimen, one may live an age; but I am not desirous of a long life.

Love me always as your best friend, the friend of your family, and as one who most sincerely wishes to see you happy.

My compliments to your dear wife, whom I wish to see as reasonable in her expences as you are:—that time will come. The happiness of this life consists in always hoping.

Rome, 30 September, 1756.

LETTER XCIII.

TO THE SAME.

YOU will see, my Friend, by the inclosed memorial of your colleagues, who tear each other in pieces, that study does not exempt us from the weaknesses incident to human nature.

Nevertheless, the learned ought to set an example of moderation, and leave quarrels and jealousies to the vulgar, as their proper element. Every age has produced literary combats very humiliating to sense and reason. The merit of one is not the same in another, and I cannot see why envy should be so exasperated as to decry those who have reputation. I would rather never have read in my life, than conceive the least

least hatred against a writer. If he writes well, I admire him; if badly, I excuse him, because I imagine he did his best.

The greater the number of mean souls who rank themselves in the list of writers, the more they detest and tear one another in pieces. Men of genius, like the generous mastiff, despise the insults of little curs. The truly great never reply to critics;—satire is best answered by silent contempt.

Men of superficial knowledge are much more exposed to these squabbles than the truly learned, because their application is quite different. The learned are too much absorbed in study to hearken to the whispers of jealousy; while the others, like light troops, are scattered about upon the watch.

The French have a great deal of these hateful disputes in their writings, from their having many more superficial than profound authors. Their agreeable vivacity, leads them to trivial studies, rather than to the study of the Sciences: from a dread

that

that their gaiety muſt be laid under reſtraint, and their liberty be loſt in intenſe application. The learned man writes for poſterity, and the ſuperficial for the preſent age; he is in a hurry to gain reputation for the immediate gratification of ſelf-love, preferring the applauſe of a day to a more laſting glory.

I am delighted to hear that your wife is become ſenſible to your remonſtrances: ſhe will poſſibly at laſt become a miſer. But take care of that, for ſhe will perhaps make you die of hunger; and a Phyſician preſcribes only ſtrict regimen to his patients.

I have ſcarce time to read the work you mention; but as you ſpeak ſo highly of its latinity, I will endeavour to glance it over. There are ſome books which I run over in the twinkling of an eye, others which I dive into ſo as to loſe nothing; but it depends upon the ſubjects, and the manner of treating them.

I love a work whoſe chapters, like ſo many avenues, lead agreeably to ſome intereſt-

interesting prospect. When I see the road crooked, and the ground rugged, I reject it at the beginning; and I do not go farther, unless the importance of the subject makes me forget the manner in which it is delivered.

I leave you to visit an English Lord, who thinks, as he speaks, with energy. He cannot conceive how Rome can canonize men who have lived holy lives; as if we did not judge of men by their lives, and as if God had not promised the kingdom of heaven to those who faithfully accomplish the law.

I believe, however, that that excellent work of the Holy Father, *On the Canonization of Saints*, will open his eyes; he esteems the Pontiff greatly, and has an high opinion of his writings. Adieu.

Convent of the HOLY APOSTLES,
5 November, 1756.

LETTER XCIV.

TO THE ABBE LAMI.

I WISH, my dear Abbé, for the honour of your country and of Italy, that the History of Tuscany, which is going to be published, may correspond with its title.

What excellent matter to handle, if the writer, equally judicious and delicate, shews the Arts springing from this country, where they had been buried during so many ages; and if he paints in proper colours the Medicis, to whom we owe this inestimable advantage!

History brings together all ages and all mankind into one point of view, presenting a charming landscape to the mental eye. It gives colour to the thoughts, soul to the actions, and life to the dead; and brings them again upon the stage of the world, as if they were still living; but with this difference, that it is not to flatter, but to judge them.

Formerly history was but badly written, and even at this day our Italian authors are not much improved. They only compile events and dates, without characterizing the genius either of nations or heroes.

The generality of men look upon history with a cursory glance, as they would at a piece of Flanders tapestry. They are content to see characters shining by the vivacity of the colouring, without thinking of the head which drew the design, or the hand which executed it. And thus they think they see every thing, while they see nothing.

It is impossible to profit by history, if we are attentive only to princes, battles, and exploits, passing in review before us; but I do not know more instructive reading, if we consider the progress of events, and observe how they were conducted; when we analyse the talents and designs of those people who set all in motion, and transport ourselves to the ages and countries in which such memorable actions happened.

History

History affords an inexhaustible fund for reflections. Every action should be weighed, not with a minute examination which doubts of every thing, but with a critical eye which will not be deceived. It is seldom that young people profit by the reading of history, because it is given to them as a kind of exercise calculated solely for the memory; instead of being told, that it is the soul, and not the eyes, which ought to be employed in such a study.

Then they will observe some men highly praised, who were the disgrace of human nature; others who were persecuted, yet were the glory of their country, and the age in which they lived. Then they will know the springs of emulation, and the dangers of ambition; they will see self-interest the *primum mobile* in cities, courts, and families.

Historians rarely make reflexions, that they may leave their readers at leisure to analyse and judge of the people of whom they speak.

In all the histories of the world, we find people who scarcely appear on the scene, yet behind the curtain set all in motion. They escape not the attentive reader, who gives them the honour of what flattery has too often afcribed to the man in office. Almoſt all princes and almoſt every miniſter have ſome ſecret agent that moves them, who is only to be diſcovered by analizing themſelves.

We may likewiſe ſay that ſome of the greateſt events which have aſtoniſhed the world, have frequently taken riſe from perſons obſcure both in rank and extraction. Many women who appeared only as the wives of princes or ambaſſadors, and who are not even mentioned in hiſtory, have frequently been the cauſe of ſome of the nobleſt exploits. Their counſels have prevailed and been followed; and the huſbands have had all the honour of enterprizes which was due to the ſagacity of their wives.

Tuſcany furniſhes much excellent matter, which an able hiſtorian might diſplay in a moſt lively and ſtriking manner. That period where we ſee princes of ſuch contracted power as the family of Medici, reviving the arts, and ſpreading them all over Europe, will not be the leaſt intereſting.

When

CLEMENT XIV.

When I reflect upon this æra, it seems like a new world rising out of chaos, a new sun coming to give light to the different nations. O that this work, my dear Abbé, had fallen into your hands! you would have given it all the spirit it is capable of. Adieu. Somebody is coming to besiege me, and I won't be blocked up;—they are visits of politeness, which should be respected.

Rome, 8th November, 1756.

LETTER XCV.

TO COUNT * * *.

I Cannot sufficiently express my joy, my dear Count, when I think you are going on steadily in the paths of virtue, and that you are sufficiently master of yourself to keep your senses, passions, and heart in order.

Yes, we will make that little excursion we projected. Your company is become my delight, since you have become a new man.

I will willingly present you to the Holy Father, when you come to Rome; and I protest to you he will be happy to see you, especially when he knows that you apply yourself to proper studies. You will find him as lively as if he was only five-and-twenty.

Gaiety is the balm of life; and what induces me to believe that your piety will be preserved, is, your being always of a chearful temper. They become insensibly tired of virtue, who become tired of themselves. Every thing then becomes a burden, and the whole concludes with sinking into a dismal misanthropy, or the greatest dissipation. I approve much of your bodily exercises; they enliven the spirits, and make us fit for every thing: I take as much exercise as the dismal profession of a monk allows.

When you come to see me, I will tell you all that the implacable Marchioness alledges in her own vindication for not seeing you. I always thought that her particular devotion would not allow her to do so good an action: she would support her conduct by vanity. You cannot imagine

imagine how difficult it is for some devotees to acknowledge themselves in the wrong.

As for you, stop where you are. You have written to her; you have spoken to her; and certainly that is enough; especially as St. Paul tells us, that we should be at peace with all the world, if possible—*si fieri potest*. He knew that there are some unsociable people in the world, with whom it is impossible to live cordially.

I embrace you with all my heart, &c.

LETTER XCVI.

TO R. P. LUCIARDI, A BARNABITE.

Most Rev. Father,

YOUR decision is quite conformable to the Councils, and I should have been much astonished if it had been otherwise, considering the long time that I have been acquainted with your extensive knowledge and your judicious opinions.

Besides the excellent books which you always have in your Library, you constantly have

have the reverend P. Gerdil, whose learning and modesty deserve the greatest praise.

Take care of your health, for the sake of religion and our own interests.

The city of Turin where you live, certainly knows the value of possessing you, for it is a place where merit is esteemed and cherished.

I make a scruple of detaining you longer from your studies and exercises of piety, and therefore conclude without ceremony by assuring you most cordially, that

I am, &c.

Rome, 3d December, 1755.

LETTER XCVII.

TO A DIRECTOR OF NUNS.

I DO not congratulate you upon your employment, but I will endeavour that you shall acquit yourself with all possible prudence and charity.

Take my advice, and go very seldom into the parlour: it is a place of idle conversation, senseless tales, and little slanders,

and

and your frequenting it cannot fail to excite jealousies; for if you see one oftener than another, they will come secretly to hear you from a spirit of curiosity, which must produce cabals and parties, and the least word you speak will have a thousand commentaries.

Secondly, you cannot remove the idle scruples you will often hear of, except by despising them, and never hearing them more than twice.

Thirdly, accustom the Nuns never to speak of any thing which does not regard themselves, while at confession, because they will otherwise make the confession of their neighbours; and in confessing one only, you will learn insensibly the faults of the whole community.

Fourthly, endeavour constantly to maintain peace in all their hearts, repeating incessantly that Jesus Christ is to be found only in the bosom of peace.

Frequently reflect, that if there is lust in the eyes of all men, as St. John tells us, there is a lust in the tongues and ears of many Nuns. Have you skill to cure them? If it is not proper to prescribe absolute
silence,

silence, it is at least necessary to prohibit malicious discourse, where they amuse themselves at the expence of their neighbours.

Respect the tenderness of the sex, which requires condescension in governing them; and shew some indulgence to the poor recluse labouring in spirit, so as not to add to the yoke, already sufficiently heavy from the burden of an eternal solitude.

Our Holy Father has known their wants, by allowing them to visit each other once a year; Whatever is done from a principle of charity deserves to be praised.

There are occasions where you will have use for all your firmness, and without which you will not be Director, but directed. Some Devotées have the address to lead him who hath the care of their consciences: they appear to do it quite piously, without seeming to intend it.

If you neglect these hints, you will repent; but you will do better if you appear only at Confession, or in the Pulpit, and at the Altar. You will be much more respected. There are few Directors who do
not

not lose a great deal by making themselves too much known. It is great wisdom never to appear among them unseasonably. Ask me nothing farther upon this article, for I have told you all that I know. Adieu.

Convent of the Holy Apostles,
19 December, 1756.

LETTER XCVIII.

TO THE COUNT GENORI.

MY books, my monastic exercises, my employment, all join to oppose the pleasure I should otherwise have in visiting you. Besides, what would you do with a Monk whose time is continually interrupted with reading and prayer, which would break in upon our walks and our conversations?

I am so accustomed to my hours of solitude and application, that I believe I could not exist without them.

All the happiness of a Monk consists in being alone, in praying and in studying. I have no other, and I prefer it to all the pleasures

pleasures of the world. The conversation of the learned or some of my friends is infinitely precious to me, provided they do not break in upon my time. I never proposed to be the slave of the minute in the hours which I can dispose of, because I hate every thing which is trifling; but I love order, and I see nothing which can preserve the harmony of the soul and the senses, but a love of order.

Where there is no order, there can be no peace. Tranquillity is the daughter of Regularity, and it is by regularity that man can shut himself up within the sphere of his duty. All the inanimate creation preach up regularity; the stars perform their course periodically, and the plants revive at the moment which is marked out to them. We can tell the instant the day should appear, and it doth not fail; we know the moment of the night, and then darkness covers the earth.

The true Philosopher never perverts the order of time, unless obliged by occupations or customs which require it.

To

To return, Sir, to natural hiſtory, which you mentioned to me: it is certain we have ſtudied it leſs than antiquity, although the former is much more uſeful than the latter. Neverthelefs, Italy at every ſtep preſents wherewithal to exerciſe and ſatisfy the curioſity of Naturaliſts. Phenomena may be ſeen in Italy, that are not to be ſeen elſewhere; and people who are ſaid to be leſs ſuperſtitious than the Italians, would inſtantly take them to be miracles.

A French Abbé, who has been here for ſome time, and whom I got acquainted with through Cardinal Paſſionei, was in the greateſt aſtoniſhment at ſeeing the wonders which nature every where preſented to him. I ſhall always remember a walk which I had with him near the Villa Mattei, and which laſted five hours, though no great diſtance, becauſe he ſtopped every inſtant. He has knowledge, and ſuch a taſte for natural hiſtory, that he glues himſelf to an inſect or a flint, ſo that he cannot tear himſelf from them. I was afraid he would petrify himſelf with looking ſo much upon ſtones; and I muſt ſay I ſhould have been

a great

a great loser, for his conversation is exceedingly engaging and chearful. This is the Abbé who has written againſt the ſyſtems of Monſ. Buffon. How much longer would he not have remained, if he had had the happineſs of being with you?

I have the honour to be with the moſt lively gratitude, and moſt reſpectful attachment,

Your moſt humble, &c.

LETTER XCIX.

TO COUNSELLOR C***.

O Such compliments! If you knew how I love them, you would not make them.

What has been ſaid with regard to the perſon in queſtion, is only founded on envy and malice. Is there a man in office, or a man who hath wrote, that has not enemies? Libels and ſatires make an impreſſion only upon weak and badly organiſed heads; and you will obſerve, that it is always the moſt vicious and ſpotted characters

which

which moſt readily believe calumny, and who ſeem to have the greateſt reluctance to ſee thoſe whom they have offended.

Prejudice, however, is ſo common, that, according to the obſervation of the Holy Father, a thouſand recommendations are wanted to determine a man in office in favour of any perſon; but there needs one word only to make him change, or to provoke him. This is the ſtrongeſt proof of the depravity of the human heart.

We ſhould be obliged to ſee nobody, were we to ſhut our doors againſt all who have been ill ſpoken of. We ought to be very careful to avoid judging raſhly. It is ſhameful to paſs ſentence againſt our brother, when we have not ſufficient proofs to accuſe him.

Prejudice ruins a number of the Great, and eſpecially Devotées, who think they ought piouſly to give credit to all the evil which is ſpoken of their neighbour. They pretend to be ignorant that God hath expreſsly commanded us not to judge, leſt we be judged; and that it is leſs criminal in his eyes, to commit faults which
they

they repent of, than to accuse their brethren rashly.

The first rule of christian charity is to believe no ill, if we have not seen it; and to be silent, if we have seen it.

Besides, if he whom they would prevent you from seeing, seeks the society of good people, it is a proof that he is not such a libertine as they pretend, or that he is inclined to reform. Perhaps his salvation depends upon the good example you will set him: therefore I would not have you reject him.

Charity does not judge like the world; because the world almost never fails to judge amiss.

I am, &c.

CONVENT of the HOLY APOSTLES.

LETTER C.

TO THE ABBE L***.

SIR,

SINCE you consult me upon the discourse which I lately heard, I must tell you with my usual freedom, that I found some excellent things in it, but did not like that affectation which enervated it. It looks like a work that had been made and painted at a Lady's toilette. For the future, let your heart speak when you mount the Pulpit, and you will speak well. Fancy should be employed only to make a border for the painting, but you have made it the foundation of your discourse.

A good Orator should keep a medium between the Italian and French, that is to say, between a Giant and a Dwarf.

Do not let yourself be spoiled by the manners of the age, or you will never be able to get rid of that affected eloquence which tortures both words and thoughts. It is of importance to a young man of abilities to receive such advice, and above all

all to follow it; and I depend upon your modesty for taking it in good part. I am with all possible desire of seeing you a perfect Orator,

Sir, your's, &c.

ROME, 10th of the Month.

LETTER CI.

TO PRINCE SAN SEVERO.

I Am always in admiration at your new discoveries. By what you have created, you have produced a second world from the first. This will distract our Antiquaries, who persuade themselves that there is nothing excellent or engaging which is not very old.

It is undoubtedly very proper that we should value Antiquity; but I think we should not make ourselves such slaves to it, as to exalt beyond measure a thing which is despicable in itself, only because it was dug out of Adrian's garden.

The Ancients had things for common use as well as we; and if they are to be valued

valued merely because of their antiquity, the earth in this quality deserves our first homage, for surely its antiquity is not to be questioned.

I neither love enthusiasm nor insensibility: those only who keep the middle between these two extremes, can either see or judge rightly. The cold indifference of the insensible, takes away all taste and curiosity; and we ought to be possessed of either the one or the other, to examine and intitle us to pronounce.

Fancy, when not regulated, is much more dangerous than indifference. It dazzles the eye, and clouds the understanding. Even Philosophy, of whom this sportive Deity should have no hold, daily feels the too fatal impression. Sophistry, paradoxes, captious reasonings, compose the train of our modern Philosophers, and have no other origin than Fancy. She takes wing as whim happens to lead, without having the least respect either for truth or experience.

Your

Your Excellency certainly knows this kind of writing, as you have frequent opportunities of reading the productions of the times. England, which on account of its phlegm we should imagine had less fancy than other nations, has often published the most extravagant ideas. Its Philosophers have been still more distracted than ours, because they must have made greater efforts to surmount their natural character of reserve and taciturnity. Their imagination is like the coal which flames, and whose vapour disturbs the brain.

It is said, with reason, that the imagination is the mother of dreams, and even produces more than the night; but these are the more dangerous, as in giving up to them, we do not think we dream, while the morning is sure to undeceive us as to the illusions of the night.

I am always afraid of your chymical experiments hurting your health, for sometimes very terrible accidents happen from them. But when new experiments in Physics are to be made, a man runs into them without any

dread

dread of the consequences, like an Officer hurried on by his valour, who throws himself at all hazards into the midst of the fire.

I have the honour to be,
With respect and attachment, &c.

Rome, 13th January, 1757.

LETTER CII.

TO A PRELATE.

My Lord,

UNITE yourself with me, that we may revenge the memory of Sextus Quintus. I was moved to a degree of warmth yesterday in supporting him against some who called him a cruel Pope, a Pontiff unworthy of reigning. It is astonishing how this character which has been bestowed upon him is supported, and what footing it has obtained in the world.

Is it reasonable to judge so great a man, without once reflecting on the times in which he lived, when Italy swarmed with robbers; when Rome was less secure than a forest, a foreſt, and modeſt women were inſulted in her ſtreets at mid-day?

The ſeverity of Sextus Quintus, who is improperly called *Cruel*, would in ſuch circumſtances be at leaſt as pleaſing in the ſight of God, as the piety of Pius V.

We have ſeen that thouſands of men have been aſſaſſinated under the reign of ſome Popes, without the murderers being brought to puniſhment: then was the time when it might have been ſaid with propriety, that the Popes were cruel: but when Sextus Quintus put to death nearly fifty robbers to ſave the lives of his ſubjects, to re-eſtabliſh morals in the midſt of the cities, and ſecurity in the heart of the country, at a time when there was neither law, nor order, nor reſtraint; this was an act of juſtice and zeal, uſeful to the public, and therefore agreeable to God.

I confeſs to you, that I mourn when I ſee great men's characters become the fable of ignorant and prejudiced writers. Even poſterity, which is ſaid to be an impartial judge, has more than once been miſled by the reflections of an artful Hiſtorian, who seats himself upon the bench without authority, and pronounces according to his prejudices.

It is in vain to cry out calumny;—the impression has been made,—the book has been read, and the multitude judge only from the first account. Thus *Gregorio Leti* has rendered the character of Sextus Quintus hateful all over the world, instead of representing him as a sovereign who was obliged to intimidate his people, and restrain them by the most striking examples of severity.

Nothing is so dreadful for a country as too mild a government. Crimes make a thousand times more victims than well-timed punishments. The Old Testament is full of examples of justice and terror, and they were commanded by God himself, who surely cannot be accused of cruelty.

I will certainly wait upon you the first moment in my power; you may depend upon it, as upon the affection with which I shall be all my life, &c.

Convent of the HOLY APOSTLES,
8 April 1757.

LETTER CIII.

TO A YOUNG MONK.

My dear Friend,

THE advice you ask about your manner of studying, ought to be suited to your disposition and talents. If vivacity is your prevailing temper, it may be moderated by reading works of little imagination; but, on the contrary, if you find your thoughts languid, you should enliven yourself by reading books written with spirit.

Do not burthen your memory with dates and facts, before you have arranged your ideas, and acquired a justness in reasoning. You should accustom yourself to think methodically, and to dispel as much as possible the chimeras that may start up in your brain.

He who thinks only vaguely, is fit for nothing, because nothing can be found capable of fixing him.

The foundation of your studies ought to be the knowledge of God and yourself.

In philofophizing upon your nature, you will acknowledge an Exiftence, to whom you owe your creation; and by reflecting on the ftrayings of the imagination, and the wanderings of the heart, you will be fenfible of the neceffity of a revelation, which hath revived the law of nature in a more lively and effectual manner.

Then will you give yourfelf up without referve to that fcience which from reafon and authority introduces us into the fanctuary of religion; and there you will attain a knowledge of that heavenly doctrine declared in the Scriptures, and interpreted by the Councils and Fathers of the Church.

Reading them will render true eloquence familiar to you, and you fhould take them early for models, fo as to fucceed afterwards in your manner of writing or preaching.

You will take the opportunity, when there are intervals in your exercifes, to caft your eye on the fineft fragments of the Orators and Poets, as St. Jerome did; that is to fay, not as a man who made them his ftudy, but as one who extracted from them whatever was best to improve his style, and to make them useful in the cause of religion.

The Historians will next lead you by the hand from age to age, and shew you the events and revolutions which have never ceased to employ and agitate the world: this will give you a constant opportunity of acknowledging and adoring a Providence which directs all according to its designs.

You will see in almost every page of history, how Empires and Emperors have been instruments of justice or mercy in the hands of God; how he exalted, and how he depressed them; how he created, and how he destroyed them, being himself always unchangeably the same.

You should read over again in the morning, what you read at night, so as to fix it in your memory; and in order to prevent your becoming a pedant, after reading a work of lively imagination, never fail to take up some more solid and phlegmatic composition.

This will compose your thoughts, which the productions of an elevated mind are apt to ferment, and will restrain the genius, which might otherwise be too easily hurried out of its proper sphere.

Endeavour to procure the conversation of learned men as much as you possibly can. Happily Providence has supplied you; for in almost all our Houses, there are Monks who have studied to advantage.

Do not neglect the society of old men: their memories are furnished with many facts which they witnessed, and which make them repositories well worth examining. They resemble old books, which contain excellent matter, though badly bound, dusty, and worm-eaten.

Be not too fond of any work, author, or sentiment, for fear of becoming a party-man; but when you prefer one writer to another, let it be because you find him more solid and truly excellent.

You ought to guard with great caution against prepossession and prejudice; but unfor-

unfortunately, the more we study, the more we are liable to be infected by them.

We become interested in an Author who has written well, and insensibly we praise and admire all his opinions, though they are perhaps very often fanastical. Guard against this misfortune, and be always more the friend of Truth than of Plato or Scotus.

Respect the sentiments of your Order, that you may not disturb the established opinions; but I do not mean that you should be a slave to those opinions. You ought not to be immoveable in any opinion but what relates to the Faith, and has been rendered sacred by the concurrence of the whole Church. I have seen Professors who would rather suffer death, than abandon the opinions they imbibed in the Schools: my conduct with regard to them has been, always to pity and avoid them. Do not apply to the scholastic erudition farther than is necessary to know the jargon of the Schools, and to confute the

Sophists;

Sophifts; for, so far from being the essence of Theology, it is only the bark.

Avoid disputes, since nothing is cleared up by wranglings: but when opportunities offer, support truth and combat error with the arms which Jesus Christ and the Apostles have put into your hands, and which consist in mildness, persuasion and charity. The mind is not to be taken by force, but to be gained by insinuation.

Do not fatigue the faculties of your mind, by giving up to immoderate study. Sufficient for the day is the labour thereof; and unless in a case of necessity, it is needless to anticipate the studies of the next day, by prolonging your application in the night.

The man who regulates his time, and uniformly devotes only a few hours to study, advances much more than he who heaps up moment upon moment, and does not know when to stop. They who are of this character, commonly end by becoming only the title-pages of books, or a library turned upside down.

Love order, but without being attentive to minute trifles; so that you may leave off till another time, when you no longer find yourself inclined to study. The scholar should not labour like an ox who is yoked to the plough, nor like a mercenary who is paid by the day.

It is a bad custom to struggle continually against rest and sleep; that which is done against the grain, is never well done; and too earnest an application to any thing injures the health.

There are days and hours when we have no disposition for application; and then it is a folly to attempt it, unless in a case of necessity.

There is scarcely any book which does not favour of painful composition in some part of it, because the Author has often wrote when he should have rested.

The great art in studying is to know when it is proper to begin, and when to leave off; without which the head becomes heated, the spirits are either absorbed or exalted, so that we produce nothing but
what

what is either languid or flighty. Learn to make a proper choice of books, that you may know only what is excellent, and to make a good use of it. Life is too short to waste in superfluous studies; and if we do not make haste to learn, we shall find ourselves old without knowing any thing.

Above all things, pray to God to enlighten your mind; for there is no knowledge without his assistance, and we are in utter darkness, if we do not follow the light which he hath revealed to us.

Dread becoming learned solely to gain a reputation; for besides that knowledge puffeth up, and charity edifieth, a Community becomes disgusted with those who make a parade of their learning.

Let events have their course, and let your merit procure your advancement. If employments do not come to seek you, be content with the lowest, and take my word for it, that is the best.

I never was more satisfied after the Chapters were over, than to find myself without any other dignity than the honour of existing: I then applauded myself for having refused all that they would have given me, and that I had only myself to govern.

The advantage of loving study, and conversing with the dead, is a thousand times greater than the frivolous glory of commanding the living. The most agreeable command is that of keeping our senses and passions in order, and of procuring to the soul the sovereignty which is due to it.

The man who is in the habit of application is a stranger to the spleen; he believes himself to be still young, when he is become old; the bustle of the cloister, like the embarrassments of the world, is always far from him.

I advise you then, my dear friend, not only for the good of religion, not only for the credit of our Order, but still more for your own sake, to acquire a habit of application. With a book, a pen, and your thoughts, you will find yourself happy, wherever you are:—Man has a certain asylum in his mind as well as in his heart, when he knows how to retire within himself.

I am

I am sensible of the singular confidence you place in me; and the more so, as you should have applied to the Fathers Colombini, Marzoni and Martinelli in preference to me. They are men whose extensive knowledge and abilities enable them to give you excellent advice. Adieu. Believe me to be your good friend and servant.

Rome, 7 June, 1757.

LETTER CIV.

TO R. P***, A MONK OF the CONGREGATION OF SOMASQUES.

My most Reverend Father,

THE loss which the Church has sustained in the person of Benedict XIV. is the more affecting to me, as I always found him an excellent Protector. I returned to Rome in the year 1740, which was the first of his Pontificate, and from that time he never ceased to honour me with his kindness. If you will make his funeral oration, you have an excellent subject. You certainly will not forget that he studied among you in the Clementine College, and that there he was initiated into that sublime and extensive knowledge, which made him one of the great Doctors of the Church, and will one day rank him with the Fathers Bernard and Bonaventure.

Take care, in this funeral oration, that your style rise with the subject, and that the magnanimity which characterised your Hero be expressed with dignity.

Endeavour to be the Historian as well as the Orator, but so as to admit of nothing dry or languid in your recital; for the attention of the Public should be constantly kept up by some great strokes worthy of the majesty of the Pulpit, and the sublimity of Lambertini.

You will in vain call all the figures of rhetoric to your assistance, if they do not present themselves of their own accord. Eloquence is only successful when it flows freely from its source, and rises from the

great-

greatnefs of the fubject: forced panegyric is not panegyric, but amplification.

From the afhes of Benedict XIV. let virtue fpring forth, and feize upon the minds of your auditors, that they may be transformed into him, and their fouls be filled with nothing but the idea of him.

Let there be no trifling detail, no affected phrafes, no bombaft expreffions. Mingle the fublime as much as poffible with the temperate, fo as to form agreeable fhadings, which will adorn your difcourfe. Be attentive to chufe a text which will happily announce the whole plan of your oration, and perfectly characterife your Hero. The divifion is the touchftone of the panegyrift, and his difcourfe cannot be excellent, if that divifion be not happily chofen.

Scatter moral reflections with difcretion, that they may appear to come naturally; that it may be faid, they could not be more happily introduced; that *there* was their proper place.

Shun

Shun all common-place;—and in such a manner, that all may see Lambertini without perceiving the orator. Praise with delicacy and with moderation, and let your praises soar to heaven, and remount towards God.

If you do not affect the soul by happy surprises and grand images, your work will only be a work of good sense, and you will have made a simple epitaph, instead of erecting a mausoleum.

Speak chiefly to the heart, filling it with those dreadful truths which detach us from the thoughts of this life, and make your auditors descend into the tomb of the Holy Father.

Pass slightly over the infant days of your Hero, for all men are nearly the same till their reason begins to shine forth. Let your periods be neither too long nor too short;—there can be no strength in a disjointed discourse.

Let your exordium be pompous without bombast, and your first sentence announce something truly great. I compare the

opening

opening of a funeral oration to the portico of a temple; and I suppose the edifice to be beautiful, if I find That majestic.

In the most forcible language shew Death overturning thrones, breaking scepters, blasting crowns, and treading the tiara under his feet: place the genius of Benedict upon the ruins, as having nothing to dread from the destroying hand of Time, and defying Death to tarnish his glory, or blot out his name.

Particularise his virtues, and analyse his writings; and every where shew the sublimity of his soul, which would have astonished Pagan Rome, as it has edified Christian Rome, and has attracted the admiration of the universe.

In a word, thunder and lighten, but manage your clouds so that the light may flash with greater splendour, and form the most striking contrasts.

My imagination kindles into flame when I think of so great a Pope as Benedict;— that Pontiff regretted even by the Protestants, and whom Michael Angelo alone could paint.

If

If I have enlarged upon this article, it is because I know that you can eafily catch the fpirit of what I recommend to you. A funeral oration is only excellent, as it happens to be picturefque, and ftrength and truth muft guide the pencil.

The generality of elogies defcend into the tomb with thofe they praife, becaufe it is only the eloquence of a day, and the production of fancy, whofe luftre is but counterfeit.

It would diftract me to fee Lambertini celebrated by an orator who is only elegant: every one fhould be ferved according to his tafte, and Lambertini's was always unerring, always good.

Engage in it, my deareft friend;—I will moft gladly fee what you throw out upon paper, being convinced that it will have fire to confume whatever is unworthy of fuch an elogy. I judge from the productions you have already fhewn me, and in which I have obferved the greateft beauties. It is time that Italy fhould forget its *concetti*, and affume the mafculine and fublime tone of true eloquence.

I endea-

I endeavour by my advice to form some young orators, who take the trouble to consult me; and I strive as much as possible to disgust them at those incongruities in our discourses, which so frequently place the burlesque by the side of the sublime. Strangers startle, and with reason, at so monstrous an alliance. The French especially are unacquainted with this unnatural medley: their discourses are often superficial, having much less substance than surface; but at least they commonly preserve an equality of style. Nothing can be so shocking as to mount above the clouds, to come afterwards tumbling aukwardly down.

My compliments to our little Father, who would have done wonders, if it had not been for his deplorable state of health.

Rome, 10th May, 1758.

LETTER

LETTER CV.

TO THE ABBE LAMI.

NO doubt, my dear Abbé, your papers are about to announce the death of our Holy Father. He was a learned man, who has a claim upon all the periodical publications, and to whom all their writers owe the higheſt encomiums.

He preſerved his chearfulneſs to the laſt; —a few days before his death, when ſpeaking of a Theatin* whoſe claim to be placed in the rank of the Saints was under examination, he ſaid, *Great Servant of God, heal me;—as you do by me, I will do by you; if you obtain the recovery of my health, I will canonize you.*

The analyſis of his works will require ſuch an abridger as you: it would be right to give extracts, that they may paſs into hands who have not time to read much, or who cannot purchaſe them in the great.

---

* One of the Order of Theatines.

Particularly, his book on the *Canonifation of Saints* fhould be univerfally known. Befides that he fpeaks as a phyfician, a natural philofopher, a civilian, a canonift and theologian, he there treats on a fubject not commonly known.

The Public imagine, that it is fufficient to fend money to Rome to obtain canonifation; while it is notorious that the Pope gets no part of it, and that every poffible means is taken to guard againft deception on a fubject of fuch importance.

This is fo true, that Benedict XIV. whofe death we bewail, being protector of the Faith, begged of two well-informed Englifhmen, who were diverting themfelves upon the fubject of canonifations, to endeavour to fhake off all prejudice, and to read with the greateft attention the verbal procefs which concerned the caufe of a Servant of God who was put on the lift of candidates for canonifation.

They confented; and after having read for feveral days with the moft criticifing fpirit the proofs and teftimonies which afcertain-
ed

ed sanctity, and all the means which had been employed to come at the truth, they told my Lord Lambertini, that if the same precautions, the same examinations, and the same severity were used with regard to all those that were canonised, there was no doubt but the matter was pushed *even to demonstration, even to evidence.*

My Lord Lambertini replied: *Well, Gentlemen, notwithstanding what you think, the Congregation reject these proofs as insufficient; and the cause of the blessed person in question remains undetermined.*

Nothing can express their astonishment; and they left Rome perfectly convinced, that we do not canonise rashly, and that there is no means easy or difficult left unemployed to come at the truth. The beatification of a Saint is a cause often argued for a whole age; and he who is vulgarly called *l'Avocat du Diable* (the Devil's Counsellor) never fails to collect all the testimonies which can be found to the disadvantage of the Servant of God, and to urge the strongest proofs

and

and moſt powerful objections to invalidate his ſanctity, and leſſen the merit of his actions.

There are a multitude of people reputed Saints who will never be canoniſed, becauſe there are not ſufficient proofs in their favour. It is not ſufficient that their virtue has been unſtained, or even ſhining; it muſt have been heroical, and perſevered in till death—*in gradu heroico* (in the higheſt degree).

Beſides this, the teſtimony of miracles is required; though unbelievers ſay, that every thing which is called a miracle is the produce of a troubled mind, or the fruit of ſuperſtition; as if God Almighty could be chained down by his own laws, without having the power to ſuſpend the execution of them; in which caſe he would be leſs powerful than the moſt petty monarch. But what truths will they not deny, when they are blinded by the corruption of the heart and mind?

God Almighty frequently makes manifeſt the ſanctity of his ſervants by healing diſeaſes;

eases; and if those miracles which are wrought after their death last only for a time, and do not continue for ever, it is because the Deity displays himself but seldom, and only to shew that his power is always the same, and that he can glorify his Saints when it seemeth good unto him.

Our Conclave is in labour; and according to custom, we cannot know till the last moment who is to be the new Pontiff. Conjectures, wagers, and pasquinades fill the whole town at present;—this is an old custom, which will not soon be left off.

As for my part, during the confusion I am in Rome as if I was not in Rome, wishing only (if it were possible) that Lambertini were replaced, and only quitting my cell for business or relaxation. It is there that I enjoy my books and myself, and regale on the reflections of my dear Abbé Lami, to whom I am an unchangeable, and most humble, &c.

ROME, 9th May, 1758.

LETTER

LETTER CVI.

TO THE SAME.

WE have at laſt got Cardinal Rezzonico, Biſhop of Padua, for the Head of the Church; who has taken the name of Clement, and will edify the Romans by his piety. It was much againſt his inclination, and after ſhedding many tears, that he could be prevailed on to accept it. What a charge for him who would fulfil the duties! He muſt dedicate himſelf to God, to all the world, and to himſelf; he muſt be ſolely employed in theſe great obligations, and have only Heaven in view, amidſt the things of this world. His dignity is the more formidable, as he ſucceeds Benedict XIV. and that it will be difficult to appear to advantage after him.

Clement XIII. continues Cardinal Archinto Secretary of State. There could be no better method of being well with crowned Heads, and of making his Pontificate

cate illustrious. He who reigns, must either choose an excellent Minister, or do all himself. Benedict XIII. was the most unhappy of men, from having placed his confidence in Cardinal Coscia; and Benedict XIV. the most happy, by having Cardinal Valenti for his Minister.

It is essential for a Sovereign, but more particularly the Pope, to be surrounded with good people. The understanding of the most clear-sighted Prince is abused, when he allows himself to be dazzled. Then copper is gold in his eyes; and be the consequence what it will, he supports those men he has once patronised.

Discernment is another quality not less necessary to Princes. There is no attempting to impose upon a Monarch who is known to be penetrating; while he who suffers himself to be led, will most certainly be deceived. There are Sovereigns who have done much more hurt by inactivity and weakness, than by wickedness. Men grow weary of doing crying acts of injustice; but are never tired of insensibility and blindness.

The

The more a Prince is weak, the more he is inclined to be despotic; because authority never destroying itself, is laid hold of by the Ministers, and they become tyrannical.

Another quality which I look upon as essential to good government, is to put every one in his right place. The moral world is governed like a game at Chess, where every thing goes on in order, according to its rank: if we place one pawn in the room of another, there is nothing but confusion.

A Sovereign is not only the image of God by the eminence of his rank, but he ought to be more so by his understanding. David, although he was but a shepherd, had a superior understanding which directed him, and which he displayed the moment he began to reign.

A Prince who is only good, is no more than what every man ought to be; a Prince who is only severe, has not that love for his subjects which he ought to have.

Alas! how excellently we atoms speak of the duties of royalty! And yet if we were clothed the dignity, we should not know how to behave ourselves. There is a great difference between speaking and reigning. Nothing resists us when our imagination takes wing, or when we allow our pen to run; but when we see ourselves oppressed with business, surrounded with dangers, beset with false friends, loaded with debts, and the most important duties, we lose our courage, and dare not undertake any thing; and by a laziness natural to all men, we trust the cares of governing to a subaltern, and are only employed in pleasures and commanding.

One thing is certain, the art of governing is attended with the greatest difficulties. If a monarch wears an hereditary crown, he knows the grandeur without knowing the management of his kingdom, and is easily deceived. If, on the contrary, he comes to an elective crown, he takes on him a sovereignty to which he has not served an apprenticeship, and appears
equally

equally embarrassed in the midst of his honours, and in the center of his business.

He who is placed upon a throne in the decline of life, is fit only to be a representative. He dares not undertake any thing; he is afraid of every thing, and he is lukewarm in every thing, especially if he is ignorant who is to be his successor. This is the situation of the Popes, if they are too old, and then they cannot attend to the affairs of church and state.

But the world will never be without abuses; if they are not in one place, they are in another, because imperfections are the natural inheritance of humanity. *There is none but the holy City,* said the great Augustine, *where all will be in order, in peace, and in charity; for there shall be the kingdom of God.*

I shall go and congratulate the new Pontiff, not as a Monk who wants to set himself forward, but in quality of Counsellor of the Holy Office. He does not know me, and I shall not put myself to the trouble of making myself known. I love to remain covered with the dust of my Cloister, and I do not think myself in the least dishonoured.

Adieu. Preserve to us always the good taste of the Medici, and your memory will be long preserved, although you care very little about it.

I am, &c.

Rome, July 5, 1758.

LETTER CVII.

TO A PRELATE.

My Lord,

THE most eminent dignity to which I have been raised by the Sovereign Pontiff, has humbled me as much as it would have elated others. I thought I was to have quitted Rome, by the manner with which they announced this very extraordinary event to me, and I have not yet recovered the surprise.

It is a reward conferred in my person on the Order of St. Francis, of which I have the honour to be a member, and I assume nothing of it to myself. My name is only lent on the occasion; for the more I reflect, the more I see, that I had neither on the side of birth, nor on the side of merit, directly nor indirectly, any claim to the Cardinalship.

If any thing can console me in the midst of the trouble with which I am agitated, it is to see myself associated with those illustrious personages who compose the Sacred College, and whose shoes I am not worthy to untie. I imagine to myself, that in participating in the credit of their virtues, I shall acquire them; and in conversing with them, I shall imitate them: we imperceptibly model ourselves by those with whom we converse. I have declared to my dear brethren, that I shall never be Cardinal to them, but they will always find me their brother *Laurence Ganganelli*; more especially as I owe to them what I am, and as the habit of St. Francis has procured me the honour of the Purple.

You know me sufficiently to be convinced that I am not dazzled by it. The soul takes no colour, and it is by the soul alone that we can have any value in the sight of God. The Lord, in making us after his own image and in his likeness, has given us more than all the dignities this world can possibly confer. It is from that view alone I can ever look upon myself as great. The Purple, all-dazzling as it is, was not made for my eyes, happily accustomed to look only towards eternity. That view wonderfully diminisheth worldly grandeur; neither Eminency nor Highness can be considered as any thing in the computation of an immortal life, where nothing appears great but God alone.

I look upon dignities only as so many more syllables in an Epitaph, and from whence no vanity can be extracted, since he who is interred is beneath even the inscriptions which are read upon his tomb.

Will my ashes have any more feeling by being qualified with the title of Eminency? Or shall I fare better in eternity, when some feeble voice upon earth shall say *Cardinal Ganganelli*,

Ganganelli, or some perishable pen shall write it?

New dignities are always a new burden, and more especially the Cardinalate, which imposes a multitude of obligations. There are as many duties to discharge, as there are occasions which require our speaking, without having any respect to aught in this world.

I shall arrange matters so as to be as little affected as possible with this strange metamorphosis. I shall, as usual, remain at the Convent of the Holy Apostles with my dear brotherhood, whom I have always tenderly loved, and whose society is infinitely dear to me.

If I quit my dear Cell, where I was happier than all the Kings upon earth, it is because I must have more room to receive those who come to do me the favour of visiting me: but I shall often say to it, *May my tongue cleave to the roof of my mouth, if ever I forget you!* I shall frequently go and revisit it, and recollect how many, very many days passed like a dream.

Thus I shall make no change in my way of life, and the dear brother Francis shall be to me in place of a whole household; he is strong, he is vigilant, he is zealous, and he will supply all wants. My person is of no greater extent, nor has grown an atom since my appointment to the Cardinalate, and therefore I do not see that more hands are necessary to serve me.

I walked so well on foot! but what comforts me is, that I shall still continue to walk on foot. I shall allow myself to be dragged in a carriage only when ceremonial requires it, and I shall become Brother Ganganelli again as often as I possibly can. We do not care to quit a way of life we have been accustomed to, especially after having lived fifty-four years in it without any trouble, and in perfect freedom.

I flatter myself that you will come and see, not the Cardinal, but Brother Ganganelli. The first will never be at home to you; but the second shall always be found to repeat to you, that whatever station I am in, I shall always be your friend and servant.

ROME, 1 October, 1759.

LETTER CVIII.

TO A CONVENTUAL MONK.

My old Friend and Brother,

I Have not yet received the packet you sent me; but I can be patient, though I am naturally very impatient. Our life is nothing but a succession of contradictions and crossings, which we must be able to bear, if we would neither disturb our rest, nor hurt our health.

P. Georgi, always an honour to the Augustines, always beloved by those who know him, has not seen the person you spoke of to me; she passed this place too quickly for him to obtain that satisfaction. She saw M. Tissot, Procureur General of the Congregation of the Priests of the Mission, whom I infinitely esteem, because he has great personal merit, and because he is a member of a body who preach to the poor with the greatest success; and lastly, because he is a Frenchman.

I muſt tell you, that I have had a very ſingular combat with myſelf ſince my promotion. Cardinal Ganganelli reproaches Brother Ganganelli for his too great plainneſs; and notwithſtanding all the reſpect which is due to the Purple, the Brother has carried it againſt the Cardinal. I love to live as I always have lived---poor, retired, and much more with my Brethren, than with the Great. It is a matter of taſte, for I am very far from aſcribing this mode of thinking to virtue.

One thing is certain: I never can put on that cold diſtant manner, as you would call it, with which perſons in office commonly receive people of low extraction who have buſineſs with them. It is enough for me, if they accoſt me, or ſpeak to me, to become the equal of my viſitor. Is it poſſible that one man ſhould affect haughtineſs towards another man, and that a Chriſtian ſhould ſtudy his expreſſions, his geſtures, his proceedings, his letters, from the dread of appearing too modeſt with his brethren? Is it poſſible that any one can refuſe an anſwer

answer to a man because he has no titles to produce? If the lowest of wretches does me the favour to write to me, I answer him instantly; and I should think myself most guilty both in the sight of God and man, if I were to omit that duty. There is no soul despicable in the eyes of religion and humanity. There is nothing so pitiful in my eyes, as a great man governed by pride.

I enlarge upon this article to let you know, that the person for whom you are interested may come whenever he pleases, and I shall be entirely his. He will be as well received by Cardinal Corsini, whose politeness corresponds with his noble extraction. If there is a fault in being too affable, it is the fault of the Cardinals. It is rare that you find any haughtiness among them; — happily there is not a stranger but does us the justice to declare it.

You will very much oblige me, by telling Signor *Antonio*, when you see him, that Cardinal Dataire will not forget his bufinefs.

Take care of your little fhare of health, by watching lefs, walking oftener, and drinking lefs coffee. It is the drink of the ftudious; but it inflames the blood, and then head-achs, fore throats, and pains in the breaft, are felt with more violence. Neverthelefs, I am no enemy to coffee; nor think of it like M. Thierry, Phyfician to the Pretender, who lives here, and is of opinion that this liquor is truly a poifon.

Your grand nephew came to fee me on Thurfday: his fpirits are as lively as his eyes. He tore one of my books in playing with it; it is to be hoped, that he will learn to have more refpect for them. He told me with great franknefs, that he would be a Cardinal. I love very much to fee the fouls of children begin to unfold themfelves: it is a bloffom which begins to open, and gives the moft pleafing hopes. He wanted to fay his Breviary with me. Alas! his innocence would have been more agreeable

able in the fight of God than all my prayers. I sent him home by my Chamberlain, but absolutely could not send him away till I had given him a chaplet:—he told me he would come again to-morrow to have another. Such things are very agreeable in a child only five years old. I wish to God he may one day resemble his father! Adieu. I embrace you in all the fullness of my heart.

ROME, 8th of the Year, 1769.

LETTER CIX.

TO A PROTESTANT MINISTER.

I Am much obliged to you, my dear Sir, for the interest you take in my health. I thank Heaven it is very good, and it would appear to me still better, if I could employ it in something more agreeable to you. The pleasure of obliging should be of all Communions.

I wish with all my soul that I could convince you, that I have all mankind in my heart, that they are all dear to me, and that

that I respect merit wherever it is to be found. If your nephew comes to Rome, as you have taught me to expect, he will find me most zealous to testify to him the affectionate regard I have for you.

My dear Sir, the Church of Rome is so perfectly convinced of the merit of the greatest part of the Ministers of the Protestant Communions, that she would congratulate herself for ever, if she could see them return to her bosom. There would be no occasion to rip up old quarrels of times past, to renew those storms and tempests, when each party, transported by passion, forsook the paths of christian moderation: but the question would be, how shall we be reunited in the same belief, founded upon scripture and tradition, such as is handed down to us by the Apostles, the Councils, and the Fathers? No body laments more than I do, the injuries that were done you in the last age: the spirit of persecution is hateful in my eyes.

What

What a multitude of people would not a happy re-union gain! If this could be effected, I would be content to die; for I would sacrifice a thousand lives to be once witness of so happy an event. That moment will come, my dear Sir, because a time must necessarily come, when there will be but one and the same faith. Even the Jews will enter into the bosom of the Church; and it is in that firm persuasion, founded upon the holy Scriptures, that they are allowed the full exercise of their religion in the heart of Rome.

God knows, my whole soul is with you, and there is nothing in the world I would not undertake to prove to you, and to all of you, how dear you are to me. We have the same God for a Father, we believe in the same Mediator, we acknowledge the same doctrines of the Trinity, the Incarnation and the Redemption, and we would both the one and the other of us desire to go to heaven. It is an established doctrine, that there are not two ways to heaven: that there should be a center of unity upon earth, as well as a Chief to represent Jesus Christ. The Church would be truly deformed,

formed, unworthy of our homage and fidelity, if it were only a body without a head.

The work of the Messiah is not like the work of men. What he hath established, ought to last forever. He has not ceased one instant to support his Church, and you are too enlightened, my dear Sir, to look upon the Albigenses as pillars of the truth to which you ought to cleave. Do me the favour to tell all your brethren, all your flock, and all your friends, that Cardinal Ganganelli has nothing so much at heart as their happiness, both in this world and the next, and that he wishes to know them all, that he may assure them of it. I can add nothing, &c.

ROME, 30th of the Year 1769.

LETTER CX.

TO COUNT ***.

I Must acquaint you, my dear friend, in the solitude where you have been for some weeks, that that Brother Ganganelli who always tenderly loved you, is become Cardinal, and that he himself does not know how, nor wherefore.

There are events in the course of human life which we cannot account for; they are brought about by circumstances, and ordained by Providence, which is the origin of all.

However it be, whether in purple or not in purple, I shall not be less yours than I ever was, but always happy to see and oblige you.

Sometimes I feel my pulse, to know if I am really myself, being truly astonished that the lot which has elevated me to one of the highest dignities, did not rather fall upon some other of my brethren, among whom

whom there are a number whom it would have perfectly suited.

All the world says, in speaking of the new Cardinal Ganganelli, It is incredible that he should arrive at such a rank, without cabal or without intrigue; nevertheless, it is very true.

O my books! O my cell! I know what I have left, but I know not what I shall find. Alas! many troublesome people will come and make me lose my time; many selfish souls will pay me dissembled homage!

For you, my dear Friend, persevere in virtue: being truly virtuous is being superior to all dignities: perseverance is only promised to those who distrust themselves, and avoid temptations; whoever is presumptuous ought to expect a relapse.

When I think how the public papers will deign to employ themselves about me, and send my name beyond the Alps, to acquaint different nations when I had the head-ach, or when I was blooded, I
shall

shall smile with contempt. Dignities are snares which have been made splendid, that people might be catched by them. Few people know the troubles which attend grandeur; we are no longer our own masters, and let us act how we will, we are sure of having enemies.

I think like St. Gregory of Nazianzen, who, when the people ranged themselves on each side to see him pass, thought they imagined him to be some uncommon animal. I own, I cannot accustom myself to this usage; and if this be what is called grandeur, I will most willingly bid it adieu. I look upon all mankind as my brethren, and am delighted when the poor or wretched approach and speak to me.

People will say that my manners are plebeian; but I do not dread that reproach, for I am only afraid of pride. It is so insinuating, that it will do all it can to penetrate and lay hold of me; but I shall contemplate the nothingness that is in me and around me, and this shall defend me against vanity or self-sufficiency.

Do

Do not think of making compliments when you come to see me; they are a sort of merchandise I do not love, especially from a friend. But here are some visitors, that is to say, every thing which thwarts me, and has rendered me insupportable to myself, for several days. Grandeur has its clouds, its lightnings, and its whirlwinds, like the tempests; I wish for the moment of calm serenity. I am without reserve, and beyond all expression, as before, your affectionate friend and servant, &c.

Rome, 3d October, 1759.

LETTER CXI.

TO CARDINAL CAVALCHINI.

Most Eminent,

YOUR recommendations are commands to me; and I shall not sleep in peace, 'till I have done what you desire. Your Eminency cannot furnish me with too many opportunities of testifying

ing the extent of my esteem and attachment. In becoming your Brother*, I become still more than ever your servant.

It would be proper that we had a particular conference upon what regards the affairs of the Church, as you are infinitely zealous for the good of Religion, which is the only object that ought to engage my attention. We are not Cardinals to impose upon the world by haughtiness, but to be the pillars of the Holy See. Our rank, our habits, our functions, all remind us, that, even to the effusion of our blood, we ought to employ all our power for the assistance of religion, according to the will of God and the exigencies of the Church.

When I see Cardinal de Tournon flying to the extremities of the world, to cause the truth to be preached there in its purity; I find myself inflamed with the noble example, and am disposed to undertake every thing in the same cause.

The Sacred College had always men eminent for their knowledge and zeal, and we should use every effort to renew the

* By his rank of Cardinal.

example. Human policy ought not to regulate our proceedings, but the spirit of God; that spirit without which all our actions are barren, but with which we may do all kind of good.

I know your piety, I know your understanding; and I am convinced, that in proper time and place, you can and will speak your mind without any dread.

Some people are endeavouring to make the Holy Father enter into engagements which he may repent of; for, since the death of Cardinal Archinto, there are no longer the same kind of men about him; and the consequences may be unhappy. The Holy See is not respected as it was formerly, and prudence requires that we should pay proper attention to times and circumstances. Jesus Christ, in recommending to his Apostles *to be simple as doves*, adds, *and wise as serpents*. An inconsiderate step on the part of Rome, in such critical times as these, may have very bad effects. Benedict XIV. himself, though he was very capable of conciliating people's minds,

minds, would have been embarraffed upon this occafion; but he would have been very cautious of infringing the rights of Princes.

What we have to treat about is delicate. There is no occafion to run counter to the Holy Father or his Council; neverthelefs we muft take meafures to prevent his being mifled by thofe about him. As his intentions are pure, he does not fufpect that he can be impofed on. He ought at leaft to balance the advantages and the difadvantages of what they attempt to make him undertake. We always fucceed badly, if we do not calculate before-hand.

The Council affect to give no explanations but to certain Cardinals, and to leave the reft uninformed. The King of Portugal will never defift from his manner of thinking, and I can fee that the other Catholic powers will fupport and confirm him in his opinions.

Monarchs no longer live detached from one another, as they did formerly; they are all friends, and act with fuch regard to each other's interefts, that if you have the misfortune to offend any one of them,

you

you will offend the whole; and inftead of having one enemy, you will have all Europe to contend with.

Shall the Holy Father, by an indifcreet zeal, ftruggle againft all the powers? Shall he fulminate againft the eldeft Son of the Church, and againft his Moft Faithful Majefty? He fhould confider that thefe are not Pagan Emperors, whom he would oppofe, but Catholic Princes like himfelf.

England fhould have corrected for ever all indifcreet zeal in the Popes. What would Clement VII. fay, were he to return upon earth? Would he applaud his work, if he was to fee that kingdom, which was formerly the nurfery of Saints, become the affemblage of all Sectaries, and every kind of error? We fhould learn to facrifice a part, for the prefervation of the whole.

The Holy See can never be more brilliant, never more fecure, never more in peace, than when it has the Catholic Sovereigns for its defenders and fupport. It is a harmony abfolutely neceffary for

the

the glory and good of religion. The faithful would be exposed to every wind of doctrine, if unfortunately the Princes wanted that deference for the Court of Rome which they ought to have; and the Sovereign Pontiff would see his flock insensibly decay, and chuse bad pasture instead of what he offers them.

The good shepherd should not only call back the sheep that have gone astray, but labour to the utmost to prevent any more from wandering. Infidelity, whose fatal blast is spread over all, does not wish for any thing more than to see Rome at variance with the Kings: but Religion abhors these divisions. We should not give room for the enemies of the Church to repeat what they have too often said, that the Court of Rome is intractable, and has a domineering spirit, which is dangerous to the other States.

The truth is, that every Sovereign is master at home, and that no foreign power has a right to command him. We thought differently in times of trouble and horror, which it would be dangerous to revive. Charity, peace, and moderation, are the proper arms of Christians, and especially those of Rome, which ought to set an example of patience and humility to all the other powers of the earth.

We should recollect, that when Peter cut off the ear of Malchus, who was an enemy to Christ, he was reproved by our Saviour, and commanded him to put up his sword in the scabbard.

How much more unjustifiable must it then appear, if such a sword was to be employed against those who have always defended, and made it their glory to be the supporters of the Holy See!

There is nothing more dangerous than an indiscreet zeal, which breaks the bruised reed, which extinguisheth the yet smoking lamp, and which would bring down fire from Heaven.

I know that a Pope is obliged to preserve the immunities of the Holy See; but there is no necessity for getting embroiled with all the Catholic Princes, on account of some seignorial rights.—This would be to ſtir up the fire of infidelity, and to give pretences for inveighing more than ever againſt the Church of Rome.

They ſee badly who ſee things but in part; the whole ſhould be examined at once, and the conſequence of the preſent proceedings weighed, to judge of the future. *One ſpark*, ſaid St. James, *will kindle a whole foreſt*.

Narrow minds imagine, that we wiſh the deſtruction of certain Monks, becauſe we will not ſupport them in oppoſition to the Kings, with whom they are at variance. But beſides that more tempeſts would ſtill follow by reſiſting thoſe Powers, we ought not to give a preference to theſe Monks, which would embroil the Court of Rome with all the Catholic Princes.

I could not poſſibly ſleep, if I was to wiſh harm to any one. I ſincerely love all the religious Orders; I wiſh from my ſoul, that the whole could be preſerved; but I reflect upon what is moſt proper, when it is become neceſſary to decide. I do not even propoſe that the Holy Father ſhould diſſolve any of them, but that he ſhould at least write to these Crowned Heads, and let them know that he will examine the complaints against that Order, and then immediately begin to make the inquiry.

Suppose Rome exposed to all these potent enemies—how can she support herself in the midst of tempests? We are not yet in Heaven; and if God preserves his Church to the end of ages, it is by inspiring those who govern it with a prudence suited to times and places, as well as with a love of peace.

It is not to be expected that God will work a miracle to defend an indiscreet zeal. He leaves second causes to act; and when an improper choice is made, things cannot possibly go well.

None but the visionary will refuse to bend to the exigency of things, when the dispute is neither about faith nor morals. In important affairs we ought always to consider how they will terminate, if we would avoid the greatest calamities.

As I know your zeal, my Lord, as well as your understanding, I presume that you will fall upon some method capable of saving,

saving, not the Holy See, which cannot perish, but the Court of Rome, which is exposed to the greatest dangers.

These are my reflections:— I persuade myself that you will find them just. I dare assure you I have weighed them before the Tribunal of God, who trieth the reins and hearts of men, and who knows that I have neither antipathy nor animosity in my heart against any man.

I have the honour to be, with all the sentiments due to your great understanding and uncommon virtues,

Your most humble, &c.

CONVENT of the HOLY APOSTLES.
16th of the Month.

LETTER CXII.

TO CARDINAL S***.

Most Eminent,

I Had not time to speak to you, yesterday, with freedom, upon the great business which at present agitates Europe, and from which Rome will receive a fatal blow, if she does not act with that moderation which Sovereigns require. The Popes are Pilots who are always steering upon tempestuous seas, and consequently are obliged to go sometimes with full sails, and sometimes to furl them, according to circumstances.

Now certainly is the time to employ that wisdom of the Serpent recommended by Christ to his Apostles. At a time when Infidelity has broken loose against every religious Order, it is certainly lamentable to see the Ministers of the Gospel forsaken, who were destined for Colleges,

Seminaries, and Missions, and who had distinguished themselves so much by their writings upon the truths of our religion; but it remains to be considered, whether in the sight of God it may be better to engage in a strife against the Powers of the earth, or to relinquish the support of any particular Order of the Church.

For my part, I think, on a view of the storm which seems to threaten us on all sides, and may be perceived already hanging over our heads, that it would be more prudent to take the necessary steps of ourselves, and to sacrifice any one of our dearest connections, rather than to incur the wrath of Kings, which cannot be too much dreaded.

Let our Holy Father and his Secretary of State regard the Jesuits as much as they will;—I subscribe with all my heart to their attachment towards them, having never had the least animosity, nor the least antipathy against any one of the religious Orders: but I shall always say, notwithstanding the veneration which I have for

Saint Ignatius, and my efteem for thofe of his Order, that it is extremely dangerous, and even rafh, to fupport the Jefuits, as things are circumftanced at prefent.

It would undoubtedly be right, that Rome fhould folicit in their favour, in quality of Mother and Protectrefs of all the religious Orders of the Church, and employ every means to preferve the Society; provided always that they fubmit to a reform, according to the Decree of Benedict XIV. and to the defire of all thofe who fincerely wifh well to religion: but my advice is, that when all thefe means have been tried, the affair fhould be left in the hands of God and of the Kings.

Rome muft always ftand in need of the protection and affiftance of the Catholic Powers. They are fortreffes which fhelter her from incurfions and hoftilities in fuch a manner, that fhe never has more glory, nor more authority, than when fhe feems to yield to thefe Sovereigns. Then it is , that they fupport her with luftre, and make it their duty to publifh every where, and

and to prove by acts of deference and submission, that they are the tractable sons of the common Father of the faithful, and that they respect him as the first man in the world, in the eyes of the faith.

The more I call to mind those unfortunate times when the Popes wandering without help, without asylum, had Emperors and Kings for their enemies, the more I feel the necessity of being at peace with all the Monarchs of the earth. The Church knows but two Orders indispensably necessary, and founded by Christ himself, to perpetuate his doctrine, and to propagate Christianity, I mean the Bishops and Priests.

The first ages of the Christian world, which we call the best ages of the Church, had neither Monks nor Friars; which evidently proves to us, that if Religion had no need of any but of her ordinary Ministers to preserve her, the Regulars, her auxiliary troops, however useful they may be, are not absolutely necessary.

—If the Jesuits have the true spirit of their profession, as I presume they have, they will be the first to say, "We will rather sacrifice ourselves, than excite troubles and tempests."

As a religious Society ought not to depend upon perishable riches, nor temporal honours, but upon a determined love towards Jesus Christ and his spouse, it ought to retire with the same alacrity it was called, if his Vicar, the Minister and Interpreter of his will upon earth, should no longer demand its services. The religious Orders are not respectable, indeed ought not to be kept up, but so long as they preserve the true spirit of the Church; and as that is always the same, independant of all the regular institutions, every Order ought to console itself if it happens to be suppressed.---But frequently vanity persuades us that we are necessary, even at those times when authority judges otherwise.

If there was less enthusiasm, and more sound principles, every one would agree in these truths; and so far from rashly support-

supporting a corps which Kings complain of, they would induce that same corps to retire of itself, without murmur or noise; but unfortunately they form an illusion to themselves, and imagine that a single institution cannot be touched, without attacking the very essence of religion itself.

If in giving up a religious Order, a dogma was to be altered, a point in morals to be corrupted; it were then, without doubt, better to perish. But the Church will teach the same truths after the Jesuits are suppressed, which she taught before they were established;—the Church will still subsist; and Christ will rather raise children to Abraham, even from the stones, to sustain his work, than leave his mystical body without succour or support.

The Head of the Church is like the master of a magnificent Garden, who lops those branches at his discretion, which, by extending too far, may happen to obstruct the view.

Do you, my Lord, who have both zeal and knowledge, confer upon these subjects with the Holy Father. It will be much more proper for you than for me, who consider myself in every respect as the least important member of the Sacred College. Shew his Holiness what an abyss he is digging for himself, when he obstinately resists these Potentates. The rectitude of his heart will make him hearken to you; for we may affirm that he has taken the resolution of resisting these Powers only because he thinks it to be right. I expect this liberal conduct from your love of the Church, and am, Your Eminency's, &c.

CONVENT of the HOLY APOSTLES,
9th November, 1768.

LETTER CXIII.

TO A LAY BROTHER.

MY DEAR BROTHER,

WHerefore do you hesitate in addressing yourself to me? Am I another man than what I was, because I have the honour of being a Cardinal? My heart and my arms shall always be open to receive

ceive my dear brethren. I owe them too much ever to forget them; for I owe them every thing.

The confession which you make of your fault, persuades me that you truly repent of it. However little a man may deviate from the straight path in cloisters, he insensibly gives into excess. You have not sinned through ignorance, and therefore you are the more to blame; and what is still worse, your fault has blazed abroad.

Humble yourself before men, and shew your contrition before the throne of grace, that you may obtain forgiveness. I shall write to your Superior to receive you again with mildness.

My dear brother, you have imagined that in quitting your retreat, you would find infinite satisfactions in the world at large. Alas! this world is but a deceiver. It promises what it never performs. Viewed at a distance, it appears to be a parterre of flowers; when nearer seen, it proves a brake of thorns.

I pray the Lord that he may touch you feelingly, for very good impulse comes
from

from him. You must resume your exercises with the most lively fervour, and oblige those to admire your reformation, who might otherways reproach you with having gone astray. You may be fully assured, that you will always be dear to me, and that I sincerely bewail with you the error you have committed. I am your affectionate, &c.

THE CARD. GANGANELLI.

CONVENT OF THE HOLY APOSTLES,
  18th November, 1760.

LETTER CXIV.

TO R. P. GUARDIAN OF ***.

IF you have any attachment to me, my Reverend Father, I pray you to receive with cordiality Brother ***, who has scandalously strayed from his duty; but he returns, he weeps, and he promises; and, what is still more affecting, Jesus Christ our model hath taught us how we ought to forgive. I pray you to

look

look upon him who was crucified for the falvation of them that crucified him; and I cannot doubt of obtaining what I defire.

Human nature is fo depraved, that I am much lefs aftonifhed than alarmed at the exceffes to which men daily give themfelves up. There needs but one emotion of pride, or a felfifh regard towards ourfelves, to make us loft to grace; and from thenceforth we become capable of every crime.

The more the Lord has preferved us from exceffes which require repentance, the more compaffionate we ought to be to thofe who furrender themfelves up to them; for our exemption is the pure effect of his mercy, and for which we fhould afcribe no merit to ourfelves.

Your flock will blefs their Paftor, when they fee with what tendernefs he again receives the ftray fheep.

I do not write to you to difpenfe with the penance prefcribed by the conftitutions, but to lighten it as much as is poffible, by abftaining from bitter reproaches,

more

more capable of irritating than affecting him.

May your reproof be friendly; may your correction be paternal; may your reception instead of being austere have nothing but what is gracious, so as not to terrify the guilty!

Remember that it is always Charity that ought to act; that it is she who ought to punish, and she who should pardon.

I embrace you most sincerely, as my o'd brother; and I hope to learn even by him whom I recommend to you, that he has found in you rather a father than a master. No body loves or honours you more than

THE CARD. GANGANELLI.

CONVENT OF THE HOLY APOSTLES,
11th December, 1764.

LETTER CXV.

TO R. P. COLLOZ, PRIOR OF GRAFFEN-
THAL, AND SUPERIOR-GENERAL OF THE
ORDER OF GUILLELMITES.

My Reverend Father,

YOUR letter expresses how much satisfaction you feel on my promotion to the Cardinalship, and of the choice the Holy Father has made of me, among all the members of the Sacred College, to trust with the protection of your * Order. I did not doubt but your sentiments, in effect, were such; nevertheless it is a matter of true satisfaction to me, to see the chearfulness which is impressed on your hearts, and to find such certain marks of the confidence with which you honour me. Your Order has certainly been deprived of a great and powerful support in losing Cardinal Guadagni. May the hopes you have conceived of me, restore peace and tranquillity to your souls! At least, I shall

* Every religious Order has a Cardinal Protector.

employ every effort, my Reverend Father, that you and all yours may find in me a tender friend, a vigilant protector, and a zealous defender of your privileges.

It is with pleasure that I frequently hear the Procureur General of the Capuchins praising your Reverence, and those of your Order.

Nothing remains to be desired, my Reverend Father, but that you will excuse me for so long delaying to answer you, which was occasioned by my having been oppressed with a multitude of affairs, that have scarce left me time to breathe, on a change so new, and so little expected on my part. I likewise beg you will put me to the proof, and see if I can be of any service to you. I have had some conversation with our Holy Father about you:--- I shall speak to him on whatever concerns your affairs, every time you chuse to employ me. I beg to recommend myself in the strongest manner to the prayers of your Order. I hope to answer your Reverence's expectations in such a manner,

as

as to convince all of you that you have in me a moſt truly affectionate Protector.

I am with all my heart,
My Rev. Father, &c.

ROME, CONVENT of the HOLY APOSTLES,
20 May, 1769.

LETTER CXVI.

TO THE ABBE F***.

IT is eaſy to obſerve, both in your writings and converſation, my dear Abbé, that you do not read the Fathers of the Church ſo much as you ought to do. Do you know that they are the ſoul of Chriſtian eloquence, and that like thoſe fertile trees which ornament gardens while they enrich them, they produce abundance both of flowers and of fruits?

The Church is proud of producing their works as ſo many monuments of victories which ſhe has gained over her enemies, and every enlightened Chriſtian ought to be delighted with reading them. The more they are examined, they will be found the

more

more conspicuously bright;---every Father of the Church has a characteristical distinction. The genius of Tertullian may be compared to iron, which breaks the hardest bodies, and will not bend; St. Athanasius to the diamond, which can neither be deprived of its lustre nor solidity; St. Cyprian to steel, which cuts to the quick; St. Chrysostome to gold, whose value is equal to its beauty; St. Leo to those ensigns of dignity which are at once graceful and majestic; St. Jerome to brass, which neither dreads swords nor arrows; St. Ambrose to silver, which is solid and shining; St. Gregory to a mirror, in which every one sees himself; St. Augustine to himself, as singular in his kind, though universal.

As to St. Bernard, the last of the Fathers in the order of Chronology, I compare him to those flowers of the velvet kind, which shed an exquisite perfume.

If the French reckon Bossuet, Bishop of Meaux, among the Fathers, it is a premature judgment, which cannot be submitted to, until the universal Church has pronounced

pronounced it, as she has the sole right of assigning the rank which is due to Writers. Even St. Thomas Aquinas has not obtained the title of a Father of the Church; and it is not to be presumed that the Doctors who have succeeded him, should enjoy that prerogative: but every nation has an enthusiasm for its Authors; yet it must be allowed, that the Bishop of Meaux was a burning and shining lamp, whose light can never be obscured.

I confess to you, my dear Abbé, if I know any thing, I owe it to the reading the Fathers, especially the works of St. Augustine. Nothing escapes his sagacity; nothing is beyond his depth, nothing above his sublimity; he contracts, he extends himself, he walks in a path of his own, varying his style and manner according to the subjects which he treats of, and always with the same advantage, always elevating the soul, even into the bosom of God; a sanctuary of which he seems to hold the key, and where he seems imperceptibly to introduce those whom he nourisheth with his sublime ideas. I particularly admire him upon the
subject

subject of Grace. Ah! I wish to Heaven, that his doctrine upon that point had been established in all the Schools, and all minds! Presumptuous writers would not then have endeavoured to found an impenetrable abyss, and the grace of Jesus Christ would have preserved all its rights, and man his liberty.

What afflicts me is, that the Fathers of the Church are scarcely read; and they who have occasion to consult them, trust to extracts, which are often unfaithful, and always too much abridged. A Priest or a Bishop made it his duty formerly to read the Fathers of the Church, as much as to say his breviary; but now-a-days they are only known by name, except it be in the Cloisters, where that excellent custom is not quite left off: whence it comes, that in many countries they have meagre theologians, without life or soul; students who can only syllogise; and instructions which contain nothing but words without meaning.

Nevertheless, I ought to say to the praise of the Sacred College, without meaning to

compliment

compliment it, that they have always had members who have perfevered in the ftudy of the Fathers; and fome may be named who actually prefer that kind of reading to all other employment.---Our Schools likewife feel that influence, where they teach only the doctrine of St. Auguftine and St. Thomas;---a certain means of avoiding whatever breathes novelty.

Let me conjure you, then, to lay it down as a rule, to read the Fathers every day; it requires but a beginning; for when once you enter upon them, you will not care to leave them: --they are always with God, and they will place you on the fame feat with themfelves, if you nourifh yourfelf daily with their writings.---It is reading the Holy Scripture to read them, for they explain it in a mafterly manner, and quote it on all occafions.

It were to deprive me of three-fourths of my exiftence, if the confolation of entertaining myfelf with the Holy Fathers was taken from me;---the more they are prefent, the more I confole myfelf, the more I rejoice, and the greater.I think myfelf.

Profit

Profit by my lessons, and you will love me if you love yourself; for in reading the Fathers, you will make acquisitions a thousand times more precious than wealth or titles. An Ecclesiastic has nothing to do with the world, but to instruct and edify it. I am with all my heart, and with the warmest desire to see your talents produce good fruit,

Your affectionate,
The CARD. GANGANELLI.

Rome, 13 December, 1768.

LETTER CXVII.

TO R. P***, HIS FRIEND.

YOU have given me a singular pleasure by not mentioning that I had written to you. Without being mysterious, I very much love discretion; and although I have been eight-and-twenty years in the Convent of the Holy Apostles, I never acquainted my brethren with what connections I have.--- They may guess, if they will,

will, or if they can; but they know nothing: *secretum meum mihi*; my secret is my own.

I lately saw the Cardinals York, Porsini, and John Francis Albani, whose excellent qualities I highly esteem; but I have learned nothing from them of what I wanted to know.

I subscribe with the greatest pleasure to all the obliging things you say of the Prelate Durini: he has joined the Italian sagacity to the pleasing manners of the French, and deserves to attain the greatest dignities.

I have learned nothing of the late resolutions of the great Personage you speak of; I see him but very seldom, and in a most reserved manner:---he does not believe me to be his friend. Is he wrong? Is he right? This is what he himself cannot decide, notwithstanding all the finesse he is supposed to be master of; but most certainly, God knows, I bear no ill-will to him, because I never have done so to any one.

I will recommend the good work which you mention, to the Cardinals Fantuzzi and Borromeo, who breathe nothing but charity. Do you yourself deliver the inclosed, which I send you for M ***, and let me have his answer by the flying Post, which is both quick and sure. For some time past my correspondences overpower me, and yet I cannot get rid of them. From this time do not lose half a page in shewing me respect: I wish you to write to me as to Brother Ganganelli. I am always the same individual, whatever efforts may be made use of to persuade me to the contrary; for, alas! if I was to attend to *etiquettes* and flatterers, they would intoxicate me with their ridiculous incense.

I love to be simply myself, and not to be beset with all the accompanyments of grandeur. Your great littlenesses disgust me; and surely they who are fond of them, must have but a contemptible spirit.

There is no probability that our common friend can recover; he has a complication of disorders, any one of which is sufficient to destroy the strongest person.

I am

I am soliciting a place which I think will suit your nephew, provided he can bear confinement, and hear grumbling; for the nobleman, whose Secretary I intend him to be, has the unfortunate madness of falling in a passion at every trifle: but his heart is not the less excellent;--- it is a blot which should be overlooked, because of his goodness. He is like Benedict XIV. who always concluded by bestowing some favour upon those he had scolded. You see that I am in a humour to prate, and that I have not the air of a man of business. When I have said my breviary, and finished my engagements, I chat more than is perhaps liked, but then I have need of it.

I leave you with yourself, that is to say, in the best company that I know; and am, as usual, and for my whole life,

Your affectionate servant,
The CARD. GANGANELLI.

Rome, 6th December, 1768.

LETTER CXVIII.

TO M. D***.

THE giving of alms is not sufficient to please God, for charity extends over all; you should not oppress your tenants, nor molest your vassals; they who with the greatest severity exact trifles which they ought to despise, have not a proper sense of religion. Christianity does not know that sordid interest, which is attentive to little things; and they have only the bark who are always upon the watch with their Tenants, for fear of being cheated. The heart is become too earthly, when it is over-anxious about worldly matters.

Ah! why torment yourself, Sir, so solicitously about the things that perish? The kingdom of Jesus Christ should have worshippers in spirit and in truth, whose hearts are not contracted by a self-interested conduct, and views merely carnal.

I am mortified when I see people of fortune living in dread of want, and though very

very rich, often much more attached to a dirty piece of gold than a poor labourer would be.

I dare add, Sir, that all your works of devotion will be absolutely useless, if you do not detach yourself intirely from the things of this world; and cease to be the tyrant of your debtors, by a greediness after riches. It is better to forego a right, than to recover it by oppression. The spirit of justice which you plead in your favour, has no connection with continual distrust, with apprehensions about future want, and with eternal wranglings.

If there are some disputes between you and your tenants, settle them more to their advantage than your own; it is conformable to the advice of Jesus Christ, who orders us, if they ask our cloak to give our coat also. All your superfluities, and even a part of your necessaries, on urgent occasions, belong to the poor; so that you will be guilty if you heap up. These are harsh truths, but the law was not made by me.

The affair you spoke to me about, could not be in better hands than Monsignor Braschi's: his rectitude is equal to his understanding, and there is no fear of his being prejudiced; nevertheless, if you desire it, I will speak a few words to him.

I am, Sir,
With the sentiments due to you, &c.
The CARD. GANGANELLI.

ROME, 21 of the present Month.

LETTER CXIX.

TO MY LORD ***.

I Have not been accustomed to see such a genius as your's become the dupe of modern philosophy. Your understanding should set you above the sophistry it engenders, and which levels us to the sad condition of the brutes.

If there is a God, as nature cries aloud thro' all her works, there must be a Religion. If there is a Religion, it must be incomprehensible, sublime, and as antient as the world,

world, as being an emanation from an infinite and eternal Being. If these are its characters, it must be Christianity; and if it is Christianity, it must be acknowledged to be divine, and heart and soul should acquiesce in it.

Is it then credible that God Almighty should display this Universe in such splendor, to feed the eyes with flocks of men and beasts, that ought to be confounded together, as having all the same destiny; and that this intelligence which dwells in us, which combines, which calculates, which extends beyond the earth, which mounts above the firmament, which recollects the ages past, and penetrates into those which are to come, and has an idea of that which ought to last for ever, should shine forth one moment, only to be dissipated afterwards like a feeble vapour?

What is that voice which incessantly proclaims within you, that you were born for great things? What are those desires which continually renew themselves, and which make you feel that there is nothing in this world which can occupy the wishes of your heart?

When man estrangeth himself from God, he is like a sick wretch rolling in agony; and the light of his reason, which he extinguisheth, leaves him in the midst of a darkness which is replete with horror.

The same truth which assures you of your own existence; I would say that intimate testimony which you find within yourself, assures you of the existence of a God, and cannot give you a lively idea of him, without impressing you with an idea of Religion. The worship which we render to the Supreme Being, is so linked with him, that our heart is not satisfied but when it is rendering homage to him, or conforming to the order which he hath established.

If there is a God, he ought naturally to be beneficent; and if he is beneficent, you ought by the justest consequence to thank him for his benefits. Neither your existence nor your health comes from yourself: about seven-and-twenty years ago, you was nothing, when all on a sudden you became an organised body, enriched with a soul to act as master, to command and guide it according to its will and pleasure. This

This reflection engages you to seek for the Author of life; and when you will examine, you will find him in yourself, and in every thing which surrounds you, without any one of these objects being able to boast of their being a part of his substance; for God is single and indivisible, and cannot therefore be identified with the elements.

If the Religion which he hath established hath taken different forms, and has been since perfected by the coming of the Messiah; it is because God hath treated it as he has done our reason, which at first was only a feeble ray; but afterwards, disclosing itself by degrees, at last appears in the brightest light.

Besides, is it for man to interrogate the Deity with regard to his conduct? Is it for a creature to regulate the ways of his Creator, and to prescribe a manner of operating to him? God communicates himself to us in part, but still reserves to himself the right of absolute dominion; because there is nothing but what is truly subject to him. If he clearly manifested his designs to us here below, if the mysteries which astonish and confound us were laid open to our view, we should have that intuitive sight which he reserves till after this life, and death would then be unnecessary. Evidence is only for Heaven, *cognoscam, sicut & cognitus sum* *: yet we would anticipate that moment, without reflecting that every thing is regulated by Infinite Wisdom, and that we have nothing to do on our part, but to submit and to adore. The unbeliever changes nothing of the designs of God, when he dares to rise up against him. He even enters into his plan, that comprehensive plan, where the evil concurs with the good for the harmony of this world, and for the happiness of the next.

Religion and nature are equally derived from God; and both the one and the other, though in different manners, have their mysteries and their incomprehensibilities; and by the same reason that the existence

---

* I shall know God, as I am known by him.

of nature is not denied, though its operations are often concealed, Religion cannot, nor ought not to be rejected, on account of its obscurities.

There is nothing here which hath not a dark side; because our soul, weighed down by a body which oppresses and darkens it, is not capable of seeing every thing. It is in a kind of infancy here below, and should have light in proportion to the weakness of its sight, till death disengages it from the oppressive load which weighs it down. It is like a tender bird which pants and cries in its nest, till it can spring up into the air, and take its natural flight.

The progress of Religion is admirable, in the eyes of a true Philosopher. It is at first seen like a twilight issuing from the bosom of Chaos; then like Aurora it announces the day; which at last appears, but surrounded with clouds, and cannot manifest itself in meridian brightness, until the Heavens shall be opened.

Hath then the unprincipled unbeliever any thing in particular which tells him, that what we believe is chimerical? At what time, and in what place has this secret light come to shine upon him? Is it in that moment when his paffions ingulph and govern him? Or is it in the midft of public fhews and pleafures, where he commonly paffes his life?

It is aftonifhing, my Lord, how men give up all the authority of tradition, and elude all the ftrength of the greateft teftimonies, to refer blindly to two or three people who give them leffons of infidelity. They will not allow of infpiration, yet they look on thofe people as oracles; from whence it may be eafily concluded, that nothing but their paffions can attach them to infidelity. They abhor a Religion which reftrains them when they would follow the torrent of their vices, and fwim in the midft of the waves of a world agitated with foaming billows.

Chriftianity is a fuperb picture traced out by the hand of God, and which he prefented to man while it was yet but fketched, till the moment Jefus Chrift came

to

to finish it, waiting the time when he should give it the lustre and colouring it is to bear throughout eternity.

Then Religion will be the only object to engage our attention, because it will be then in the essence of God himself, making, as St Augustine expresseth it, *a whole with him.*

This progress is conformable to that of the time which constitutes this life, and which does not exist but by succession. God has thus varied the forms of Religion, because we are in a variable world; but he will fix it unalterably in Heaven, because there no change will be known. These are the combinations and proportions which display the wisdom of the Supreme Being. Religion being for man, it was his pleasure that it should follow the progress made by man, according to the different modes of his existence.

They who are intent upon this world, see nothing of all this; but you would judge of these things as I do, if you were disengaged from all the pleasures and all the riches which make you a materialist,

in

in spite of yourself. Christianity is spirit and life; and they stray widely from it, who are occupied only about what is corporeal. Souls become enlightened at death, only because they are no longer weighed down by bodies which besiege and darken them. True philosophy, in disengaging man from whatever is carnal, does what death will finally effect; but it is not the modern philosophy, which acknowledges no existence but that of matter, and looks upon metaphysics as a science purely chimerical, although much more certain than physics, which has only its existence in the senses.

I do not enter into the proofs of Religion, because they have been so often and so well explained already in immortal works, that I could only repeat them. Jesus Christ is the beginning and the end of all things, the key of all the mysteries of grace and nature; so that it is by no means surprising that we should stray after a thousand absurd systems, when we do not steer

by

by that sublime Compass. I cannot give you a reason for any thing in physics or in morals, as Cardinal Bembo wrote to a Philosopher of his time, if you do not admit of Jesus Christ. Even the creation of this world is inexplicable, incomprehensible, and impossible, if it was not effected by the Incarnate Word; for God can have no other intention in what he does, but what is infinite. This is the reason why St. John called our Saviour *Alpha and Omega*; and that the Apostle told us that the ages were made by him: *Per quem fecit et sæcula.*

Study, then, as much as a creature is capable, this Man-God, and you will find all the treasures of science and wisdom in him; you will observe that he is the first link of that chain which bindeth all things visible and invisible; and you will acknowledge him to be that divine breath which inspires justice and holiness into all hearts.

The unbeliever can never give a satisfactory answer, when you ask him, Who is
this

this Jesus Christ, this Man at the same time so simple and so divine? so sublime and so humble? so pure in the whole course of his life? so great in the moment of his passion? so magnanimous at his death? But to answer this question without evasion. If he is only a man, he is an Impostor; for he hath said he was God; and from that time, what becomes of his sublime virtues? what becomes of his Gospel, in which he forbids the use of the least equivocation? and how account for his disciples victories in all parts of the world? And if he is a God, what ought we to think of his religion, and those who dare to combat it?

Ah! my Lord, behold what is better to know, and better to examine, than all the profane sciences which you study. Sciences will be at an end: *Linguæ cessabunt, scientia destruetur**; and there will be nothing but the knowledge of Jesus Christ, which will ride triumphant upon the abyss, when time and the elements shall be swallowed up.

* Languages shall cease, and Science be destroyed.

Consider

Consider but yourself, and that view will necessarily lead you to truth. The smallest motion of your finger declares the action of God upon your body; this action announces a Providence; this Providence informs you that you are dear to your Creator; and this information leads you from truth to truth, till you come to those which are revealed.

If you are neither the creator of yourself, nor your own ultimate end, you ought necessarily to search for Him in whom these two qualities subsist. And what can that be, if it is not God?

Religion will be always sure to gain her cause in the eyes of all those who have principles. It is sufficient to remount to its source, to analyse and investigate the ends of its institution, to come at the truth: but the wicked dishonour and disfigure it, and substitute a skeleton in its place. I am not surprised, then, that they who are not instructed, and who put their trust in the false philosophy of the age, should look upon it as a bug-bear.

My

My Lord, I expect from the rectitude of your soul, and the extensive powers of your mind, a more solid judgment than what you have hitherto held with regard to Christianity. Shake off all these systems, and all the opinions with which you have been unfortunately biassed; enter like a new man into the way which tradition will open to you, and you will judge very differently; appeal from your prejudices to yourself; for as yet it has not been yourself that has pronounced any opinion upon this subject. As for my part, I say what my heart and soul dictate to me, when I assure you of all the affection with which I shall remain, during life,

Your servant, &c.
The CARD. GANGANELLI.

ROME, 29th November, 1768.

LETTER CXX.

TO COUNT * * *.

THE reflexions which you have made upon the present state of the different courts of Europe are very judicious. It is plain that you know them perfectly; and though you are not of their cabinets, you are very well acquainted with what is passing there.

It is well to be on a level with the age, to know it perfectly, and to observe the springs which move the great personages who figure on the stage of life.

The person you speak of *is a man of wool*, without consistence or steadiness, and upon whom, consequently, there can be no dependence. There is another person you know, zealous as he ought to be for the August House of Bourbon; but though he leaves his Palace with a firm resolution to speak strongly to the Holy Father about the affair of Parma, he is scarcely got into

to his presence, when awe renders him speechless. As to the little Prelate who should act and constitute himself Mediator, he is an indecisive person, who is always putting off every thing till the morrow, and who has no other answer but *Vederemo*, We shall see.

We might easily speak about it to the General of ***; but it is not safe to confide in him at present; especially when even the secret enjoined by the Holy Office is not kept. As to his Assistant, he is merely a well-meaning man.

Many of the great men here are with reason attached to France and Spain; but they dare not explain themselves, they are so teazed and beset by numbers, who make Heaven speak as they please.

A devotion faintly enlightened, which is unhappily but too common, is constantly whispering, that all should be sacrificed to defend the interests of God; as if God required that his First Minister upon Earth should embroil himself with all the Catholic Power, to support some seignorial rights;

rights; and, at all adventures, to preserve a Corps, which can be of no further utility, when the tide of prejudice runs against it.

Let us suppose, for a moment, that there is nothing against them but prejudice; nevertheless, it is certain, that they can be no longer useful, when opposed by powerful Princes; but it is impossible to make people bear reason upon this subject, who have adopted a certain manner of thinking.

All this forms a labyrinth, from whence we can see no exit; and the best way we can take, is to be silent, and wait God's good time. When he pleases, he can enlighten their minds, and make them know his intentions.

The evil is, that the longer they are kept in suspence, the more they are inflamed. I am persuaded, Monf. the Count, notwithstanding all the talents which I know you possessed of, that you do not see an easy means of extricating us out of this confusion. We have to do with people who loudly exclaim against all propositions

of

of accommodation; and it is impossible to say any thing to them, because they fancy themselves to be inspired.

Nevertheless, I cannot help being greatly offended at some discourse that certain persons hold against Clement XIII. especially as it is not permitted to speak against the High Priest, and that we read in the Epistle of St. Jude, that St Michael durst not utter curses even against the Devil; but that he was content to say, The Lord rebuke thee: *Non est ausus judicium inferre blasphemiæ, sed dixit: Imperet tibi Dominus.*

From hence I conclude, that the generality of men, be their manner of thinking what it will, bend Religion to their prejudices. Some are great friends to the Religious Society which is the subject of the present disputes, while others are equally its enemies; and the consequence is, that things are not seen as they ought to be, and that truth can no longer be heard amidst the clamours of passion. For my part, who always keep in the middle between the two extremes of parties, and deteſt cabals and prejudices, I think that the Pope can do nothing better, than under the guidance of God to examine all the papers both for and againſt them, as likewiſe all the inconveniencies which reſult either on the one ſide or the other, and then he can and ought to pronounce; for he is Judge; and I never pretended that he was the ſimple Miniſter of the will of Princes. None but he who eſtabliſhed a Religious Order can deſtroy it; but he has ſuch a right, as it would be madneſs to diſpute with him.

What comforts me amidſt all theſe evils, is, that though the bark of St. Peter muſt always be agitated, the Lord likewiſe will ſupport it, even in the midſt of the greateſt tempeſts. You are ſurely more perſuaded of theſe things than any men; you, Sir, who have always made eternal truths the object of your meditations, and have ſeen whatever has any relation to Religion with the eyes of the Faith. Theſe eyes, far different from thoſe of Philoſophy, raiſe

us

us above this world, and give us to range in the divine immensity. There can be nothing therefore so absurd as to say, with the modern Philosophers, that the views of Christians are extremely limited. Can a soul be contracted in its ideas, when it extends its thoughts even to eternity, and, rising above the Universe, approaches to God himself, a pure and immaterial Spirit?

In drawing a parallel between Religion and Philosophy, it will be immediately perceived, that the former gives a boundless extent to all the faculties of the Soul; and that the latter contracts them within a very narrow circle. This world is the *ne plus ultra* of the Philosophers of the present times; but with the Christian, 'tis only an atom. The one makes it his happiness and his end; the other looks upon it merely as a shadow which passeth away, and regardeth it only with a glance of his eye. This adores it, because it is his all and his God; that looks upon it as a vapour, which will very soon be dispelled.

Do not reckon upon the Prelate ***; he is too busy.

If any change happens here, I shall be ready to acquaint you with it. But there must be a terrible concuſſion for That to take place. I have the honour to be, Monſ. the Count, &c.

My Compliments to M. the Abbé.

LETTER CXXI.

TO A PRELATE.

YOU have very senſibly obliged me by the ſervices you have done the Reverend Father Aimé de Lambale. He is a Capuchin whom I ſingularly love for his good qualities. He has the virtues of his profeſſion; that is to ſay, he is humble, gentle, zealous, and gives great application to preſerve the rules of his Order in their full force.

I expect your return with impatience, eſpecially as the ſubject of our converſation will

will be some people's readiness to talk, and backwardness to execute.

Every day brings us some very extraordinary news, which the next day contradicts it. When the spirits are in a ferment, and affairs of consequence are in agitation, every one sets up for a politician and news-monger; more especially in Rome, where we have so many idle speculators.

Some have fears, others have hopes, this life being only a succession of disquiets and desires. It was given out yesterday, that the King of Naples had marched some of his troops into our neighbourhood.

St. Ignatius, who was inflamed with zeal for the glory of God, did not foresee the strife which his children would one day occasion. It is said, nevertheless, that he begged of God they might always be sufferers. If that be the case, he has certainly been heard; for it must be allowed, that for some time they have undergone a number of calamities. I have been really exceedingly

-ceedingly affected by their misfortunes;—they are my brethren, by the double title of Men and Monks: *and if thefe things are done in the green tree, what will be done in the dry? Quid in arido fiet?*

You will no longer find your Director here. We have buried him. This fame Death, who generally comes without being called, gives us no refpite. He goes his rounds day and night, and yet we live in as much fecurity as if we thought he would never come near us.

I flatter myfelf that you will bring me the little picture which I requefted of you. Depend upon my efteem and friendfhip: it is all that I can give you, but I give it amply, being, &c.

ROME, 23d April, 1768.

LETTER

LETTER CXXII.

TO THE MARQUIS OF CARACCIOLI.

SIR,

I Return you a thousand thanks for the book you was so obliging as to send me, and which has for its Title *Les Derniers Adieux de la Marechale à ses Enfans:* It is sentimental, and makes such lively impressions upon the heart, that I was very deeply affected with it. You should give it to us in Italian; and the rather, as I look upon it to be a complete treatise on education.

I am sorry that you was not provided in time with all the interesting anecdotes of Benedict XIV. You were too late in setting about it. When there is an intention of publishing the history of a Sovereign Pontiff, memoirs should be collected while he lives; every one is then anxious to give them; whereas after his death he is immediately forgotten, and frequently even by those who owe their fortune to him.

I advise

I advise you, Sir, to continue your literary pursuits, which are so beneficial to the Public, provided you do not injure your health by it; and to believe that I am, more than I can express,

Your affectionate Servant,
THE CARD. GANGANELLI.

ROME, 13th September, 1768.

LETTER CXXIII.

TO THE AMBASSADOR OF ***.

IF the affairs of Parma, like that of the Jesuits, had any connection with the Faith, there could be no temporising, accommodation, nor capitulation; because the answer from the Popes to him who would change his Faith is, *You must rather die.*

One thing only is certain, I am afraid that the Kings will at last do just what they please, and that we shall be forced to yield at a moment when all submission may be rejected.

Rome is no longer in thofe times, when men of all ranks brought her their vows and offerings; yet, were fhe ftill in the fame fituation, could fhe confcientioufly infringe upon the rights of Kings? A Pope ought undoubtedly to preferve all his immunities; yet not fo tenacioufly as to hazard fo dangerous a fchifm—Nothing is fo much to be guarded againft as dividing the body of Chrift's-Church.—Rome is the center of unity, and ought not, therefore, for articles which neither affect Morals nor the tenets of Religion, to provoke thofe who live in her bofom to feparate from her.

If, when the Kings began to complain of the Jefuits, the General himfelf had written to thofe Monarchs to foften their anger, and to defire that the offenders might be feverely punifhed;—if the Holy Father himfelf had followed this plan, the Kings might have been appeafed; and I truly think it would have fucceeded, provided a reformation had been offered. But they were obftinate, and ftill perfift with the fame pertinacity to fupport the Society:

Society: and this is what stirs up so many people against them.

P. Pontalti, General of the Carmelites, was an excellent Politician, when he wrote to the King of Portugal to beg that he would prevent his Monks from trading to Brazil. He advised R. P. Ricci to take the same step, but he would not listen to his counsel.

Where is the Sovereign who may not, in his own kingdom, either protect or expell such as offend him? I dare say, that the acting Minister did not take this affair rightly, and did not foresee all its consequences: *there are fine eyes that see nothing.*

The example of Avignon, Benevento, and Porte Corva, shews us, that if there is not an immediate accommodation, some other places will be seized; and thus insensibly we shall lose territories to which long possession had given us an indubitable right.

Benedict XIV. although timid, would have satisfied the Kings in this crisis; and it is unfortunate that things are seen in a different light by Clement XIII. whose piety we respect, as well as that of the Cardinal his nephew. I ventured to speak to him on that subject, and he was struck with what I said; but immediately, some people who were interested in keeping up the opinions which they had suggested to him, came in the way, and gave him some specious reasons for persisting in his sentiments. They said, that a religious Order which had done the greatest services in both worlds, and had made an express vow of obedience to the Holy See, ought absolutely to be preserved; and that it was only from a hatred to Religion that there was an attempt to destroy it: but they did not tell him, that, as the common Father of all the Faithful, he ought not to provoke the Princes who were the most religious, and the most obedient to the Holy See; nor did they tell him what might be the result of a schism between the Holy See and Portugal; and that the Head of the Church should tremble, when a separation is threatened which may have the most fatal consequences.

There

There is nothing in losing some little portion of territory, in comparison with the souls which may be lost by a schism. What a lesson would England afford to Clement VII. if he was alive at this day! It makes one shudder with horror. Certainly the Sovereigns who reign at present will never think of a separation; but can we answer for those who are to succeed them? It is not always what presents itself under the idea of piety, that is the most expedient measure.—A Pope is established the Head of the Church, that he may root out as well as plant. The good books which the Jesuits have left us, will live after them. The religious Orders have not been gifted with infallibility nor *indefectibility:* if they were all to be abolished this day, undoubtedly the loss would be great; but the Church of Jesus Christ would neither be less holy, less Apostolical, nor less respectable. The religious Societies are upon the footing of auxiliary troops; and it is the great Pastor who is to form a judgment when they are useful, and when they are no longer so.

The Humiliars, and even the Templars, did good for a time, becauſe there has been no Order but what has edified, eſpecially at the beginning of its inſtitution; yet they have been ſuppreſſed when the Kings and Popes found it neceſſary.

Certainly I muſt regret the good which the Jeſuits might have done; but I ſhould regret much more the kingdoms that might have ſeparated from us on their account.—Theſe Fathers themſelves ſhould feel the juſtneſs of my reaſonings; and I have the preſumption to believe, that I could make them acknowledge it, if I had a conference with them, and they would ſhake off the prejudices which are attached to all conditions of life. If my friend P. Timoné had been their General, they might probably have ſtill ſubſiſted.

This is my way of thinking, though of a religious Order myſelf; and I would conſent to the diſſolution of my own Society, if I found it obnoxious to the reſentment of the Catholic Princes.

There are, happily, certain devotions which have never dazzled me. I weigh the events

events according to Religion and equity; and as these are two certain lights, I shall ever be determined as they direct me.

If there were no other interest in the Church but that of Jesus Christ, all the Faithful would wait in peace for the events marked out by Providence, without engaging warmly either for Cephas or Apollos. But we are only guided by sensible affections; and because we have once known a Monk who has edified by his conduct, and who has taught nothing but what was excellent, must we therefore conclude that we neither can, nor ought to suppress the Order of which he was a member?—Is this to reason, or is this to judge?

When we have neither seen the informations nor the arguments upon which we should frame a judgment, it is absurd to attempt to pass sentence. Here is a great contest between Kings and a religious Order eminent for its talents and credit:—when we do not know the motives from which they act, we neither can nor ought to pronounce an opinion. I say once more,

more, that I do not affert that the Jefuits ought to be fuppreffed, but I think that the complaints of the Kings fhould be attended to; and if there are ftrong reafons for it, that then the Order fhould be abolifhed.

We do not as yet know precifely the reafons for the deftruction of the Templars, and yet there are people who would know already the motives which have caufed the fuppreffion of the Jefuits. I wifh with all my heart that they may be able to juftify themfelves, and that there may be neither divifion nor diffolution; for I have a foul truly pacific, and incapable of hating any one, and more particularly a religious Order.

I have the honour to be, &c.

Rome, 29 October, 1768.

LETTER CXXIV.

TO THE MARQUIS OF ✶✶✶.

BEHOLD us in the greateſt criſis we ever were in! All Europe thundering againſt us, and unfortunately we have nothing to oppoſe to this raging tempeſt. The Pope truſts in Providence; but God Almighty does not work miracles every time he is called upon; nor can we expect that he will interpoſe his power, merely that Rome may maintain a right of ſeignory over the Dutchy of Parma.

Rome has no adminiſtration but what is purely ſpiritual in the Roman Catholic kingdoms, and it is only in the Eccleſiaſtical State that ſhe has any temporal authority; and even That is owing to the conceſſion of thoſe Sovereigns whom we are ſolicited to oppoſe.

The Court of Rome cannot forget that ſhe owes almoſt all her riches and ſplendor to France; and if ſhe does remember it, how can ſhe avoid compliance with the de
ſire

sire of Louis XV. especially as he only asks those things which he has a right to exact?

I compare the four kingdoms that principally support the Holy See, to the Cardinal virtues; France to Strength, Spain to Temperance, &c.

The Holy See thus defended, shews herself formidable to her enemies, and then may we say; *Cadent à latere tuo mille, & decem millia à dextris tuis; ad te autem non appropinquabit* *.

I own to you, my dear Sir, that I grieve at the sight of the dangers which seem to threaten us, and I most heartily say,— "May this bitter cup be put far from us!" Not because they take our cloak, and can take our coat also; but because I dread a rupture, and the multitude of evils which may follow, although Religion can never perish!

If the Holy Father, whose heart is purity itself, would only represent to himself the benevolent acts of the French Monarchs

---

* A thousand shall fall at your right, and ten thousand at your left; and no evil shall approach you.

to the Holy See, he would not hesitate to comply with the desires of Louis XV. touching the Dutchy of Parma; but you know that every thing has two faces, and that the aspect under which some people present this affair to our Holy Father, is absolutely contrary to the views of the Sovereigns.

He will find the necessity of retreating; at least, if the present Pope does not, his successor must; which will be the more unlucky, as Clement XIII. is a Pontiff worthy of the first ages of the Church for his piety, and deserves to be blessed by all the kingdoms who acknowledge his authority.

The Sacred College might remonstrate to him; but beside its being divided in sentiments about the affairs of Parma and the Jesuits, the Pope will do nothing which is not advised by his Council.

I am not at all surprised that Cardinal *** should so warmly interest himself for the Society and its General; there are reasons quite natural for his attachment: but I am surprised at his being consulted in preference, considering that all the world knows his sentiments already

upon

upon the subject. In critical circumstances, the opinions of those who are totally disinterested ought only to be taken; otherwise we become without intending, or even suspecting it, partizans.

It is right to love only Truth, and to know her such as she is; so many illusions assume her appearance, that we are often deceived. When we would see her without a cloud, upon occasions which present themselves, we should divest ourselves of all we already know, and seek information as if we were totally ignorant of the matter; taking the advice of those who see and judge without prepossession.

Besides this, we ought to have a rectitude of intention, by which we should deserve to obtain supernatural lights; for the Lord trieth our hearts and reins; and if we are not animated with a love of justice in our researches, he abandons us to our own blindness.

I am, in all the fulness of my heart, &c.

ROME, 7th January, 1769.

LETTER

LETTER CXXV.

TO A MONK OF HIS OWN ORDER.

PROVIDENCE, in raising me to the Cardinalship, has not made me forget from whence I rose; it is a view which is always present to me, and I find it excellent to defend my mind from vanity. The dignity which I possess, and to which I was not born, has more thorns than roses, and in that resembles all eminent stations.

I am often obliged to be of a contrary opinion to the person in the world whom I respect the most, and who likewise deserves all my gratitude. It is the most cruel combat that my heart can sustain.

Charity, inseparable from truth, has not always the most pleasing things to say; but many people are deceived upon this subject, imagining that it ought to be always gentle, and always complying:—in that case it would resemble flattery. There are circumstances where charity flames, lightens and thunders. The Fathers of the Church who

who were filled with this spirit, when they spoke with the most anxious zeal, spoke with a voice of charity.

When you write to the Bishop of ***, make my most sincere compliments to him, and tell him, that every means has been employed to bring about an accommodation; but to no purpose. God will sooner or later make manifest his will, for we ought never to lose sight of him.

You restore me to life, by telling me that our common friend is likely to recover. His understanding is of great use to those who consult him. He has an excellent talent for guiding, without having the littleness of the major part of Directors; for it must be owned, that many men who direct, have need themselves of being directed, as they are almost always ruined by women, who pay them a reverence due only to their God.---They look up to their spiritual Guide, as if he was the Archangel Gabriel at least. It is undoubtedly right that they should have an esteem for those they consult, and whom they hear as the

oracles

oracles of the Law; but that esteem should not be carried to excess.

They who have a continual enthusiasm for their Directors, may be persuaded that some motives of a mere human nature have mixed themselves up with such an attachment.

What a surprise will it be for a number of Devotees, who, believing themselves sincerely devoted to God, are only the worshipers of their Directors, and who will hear that dreadful sentence pronounced at the moment of their death, from the Supreme mouth, "As I have not been the ob-"ject of your love, *depart, I know you not:*" *Discedite, nescio vos.*

This is what I have long shuddered at, on the article of Directors. I could have wished that he who was formerly mine at Rome, and who died in the odour of sanctity, had made his manner of directing public. He was a heavenly man, who raised us above humanity, and wished to make us absolutely forget himself, and
every

every thing elfe, but what attached us to God alone.

We want a good book upon the subject of Direction in Italy. We have a multitude, but they are only filled with commonplace. To compose a good one, there wants, in the first place, the spirit of God; secondly, an extensive knowledge of the human heart; for it is incredible with what addrefs vanity, and a thousand affections of the senses, infinuate themselves at a time when we are persuaded that our sentiments are sublime and worthy the attention of the Eternal. This is the reason of the great difficulty in judging of ourselves.

I wish you every thing that you can desire, because I know that you desire nothing but what is most excellent; and I am your dearest and most affectionate servant,

The CARD. GANGANELLI.

CONVENT of the HOLY APOSTLES.

LETTER

LETTER CXXVI.

TO COUNT DE ***.

WE are at laſt ſummoned to a Conſiſtory, which is to determine great things. We are to deliberate upon thoſe unfortunate buſineſſes which have embroiled us for a conſiderable time with the Catholic Powers. It is probable, that the Holy Father, finding at laſt that he is not in a ſituation to reſiſt, will acquieſce in the requiſitions of the Houſe of Bourbon. He will at leaſt lay the reaſons of his diſſent before us for our conſideration, and every one will give his opinion.

I wiſh to God they had followed that plan from the beginning! But we do not often ſee the conſequences of a troubleſome affair till we are engaged in it.

I adviſe you to confer with ———; Rome, though renowned for politics, is not always ——— you underſtand me.

The Miniſters continue to make the moſt bitter complaints; and the intereſted parties,

parties, that nothing may be concluded, form circumvallations, blockades, and ———. your own sense will tell you the rest.

There is every reason for presuming that France, Spain, and Portugal will, &c.

I will tell you nothing, if silence is imposed upon me, and certainly you will approve my conduct. I will not expose myself to the same reproaches with the little man in question, for having betrayed secrets.

Beside the probity of a Cardinal, I have that natural rectitude which makes the essence of an honest man, and which is a double engagement to be discreet: but all of us shall not be sufficiently so, for I suspect the affair will be instantly divulged; and I shall not be surprised if the writers of the Dutch Gazettes should be informed of all.

I can know nothing before-hand, because nothing is declared. The life which I lead here is of as dark a complexion as my habit, and consequently I am not to be found in those brilliant circles where

great

great news is the subject of conversation. I only learn things by the means of our dear Abbé ―――. But does he know every thing, and always speak truth? It is not because he means to deceive, but his imagination, his vivacity, &c.

I have again seen the Flying Post ――; He has sent me the letters I expected, and they contain nothing but wise reflections upon what I wanted to know. Adieu without ceremony, as you desired.

Rome, 31 January, 1769.

LETTER CXXVII.

TO THE SAME.

HERE is quite another affair on our hands than the Consistory I mentioned to you last post. The Holy Father, on going to-bed last night, was seized with a violent convulsion, uttered a great cry, and expired. We were to have met as this day, and to have drawn from the alembic that which keeps all the Catholic Courts

Courts in fufpence, and has occafioned our being upon bad terms with them. Every one will reafon differently upon this death, which has happened fo extraordinarily in the prefent circumftances.

I fincerely regret the late Pope, on account of his excellent qualities, and the gratitude which I owe him. Religion ought to make his encomium, and bewail the lofs. He made himfelf truly refpectable to all who approached him, by his moft pleafing manners, which were pure as his intentions, and by a muft incorruptible zeal: but I fhall always fay, that it was a pity he did not view things in their proper light.

He has left fome Nephews deferving of the higheft commendation by their excellent qualities, efpecially the Cardinal, who is one of the beft men in the world.

The great difficulty now is, to know who will be chofen. I pity him before-hand, and I do not think it is right for me to fay to you, that it will be Such or Such-a-one; for it is often the perfon who has been leaft thought of. One thing is certain, that I will not give my voice to any, but one in whom knowledge is joined with piety. A Pope, as Vicar of Jesus Christ, ought to have true devotion; and as a temporal Prince, a great deal of knowledge and sagacity. Happily, the Sacred College has many among its Members whom we may chuse with propriety. Pray that the Lord may inspire us, and give us a Chief according to his own heart, and the hearts of the Kings.

I have lately seen M. Marefoschi: he is a Prelate that deserves to be esteemed for his knowledge and candour.

The Conclave will be now more tolerable than in summer. It will make no great change in my way of life. It is only quitting one cell to go into another: and if they have intrigues, I protest to you I shall know nothing of them, being the man in the world who meddles the least in party-matters.

You know my heart, and I need not say to you that I am, &c.

Rome, 3d February, 1769.

LETTER CXXVIII.

TO A MONK, ONE OF HIS FRIENDS.

I AM going to the Conclave. Pray to God that he may bless our intentions, and restore a calm to us, after so long a storm.

I have been pressed to take a French Conclavist*. Besides that I very much love his nation, he has some excellent qualities; however, I will depend upon myself, that I may have nothing to fear from his indiscretion, if I should accept him, and he should be inclined to blab: *Secretum meum mihi*; My secret is my own.

Tell our Prelate that I could not answer his letter, but that I expect himself at the Convent of the Holy Apostles, the day the Conclave breaks up. Minds are divided, but God can do what seemeth to him good, and it is his work that we are to be employed in.

* A Cardinal's Secretary while in Conclave.

Endeavour to procure for me the book I spoke of, against the moment I recover my liberty. Adieu!

I am always your Friend and Servant.

SIX IN THE MORNING.

LETTER CXXIX.

TO MONSIGNOR ✱ ✱ ✱.

FOUR months are past, in which time I have not existed either to myself or my friends, but to all the different Churches, of which, by the Divine Permission, I am become the Head; and to all the Catholic Courts, several of whom, as you know, have very important affairs to regulate with the Court of Rome.

It was impossible to become Pope in more litigious times, and Providence has permitted the oppressive load to fall upon me. I hope that the Divine Grace will support me, and give me the strength and prudence which are indispensably necessary to govern according to the rules of juſtice and equity.

I endeavour to take the moſt exact cognizance of the affairs which my Predeceſſor left me, and which cannot be finiſhed but after a long examination.

You will do me a very great favour, if you will bring me what you have wrote upon the things which relate to this ſubject, and to truſt them to myſelf alone.

You will find me, as you have always known me, as much a Stranger to the grandeur with which I am ſurrounded, as if I knew not even the name; and you may ſpeak to me with the ſame frankneſs you uſed to do formerly, becauſe the Popedom has given me a new love for truth, and a new conviction of my own nothingneſs.

ROME, 24th September.

LETTER CXXX.

TO A PORTUGUESE LORD.

YOU need not doubt of my having all possible desire to unite, more closely than ever, those ties which have been attempted to be broken between the Courts of Rome and Portugal. I know how intimate a connection has always subsisted between these two Powers, from the earliest times, and shall be happy to place things on their old footing; but, as Common Father of the Faithful, and as Chief of all the religious Orders, I shall do nothing until I have examined, weighed, and judged, according to the laws of justice and truth.

May God forbid that any human consideration should influence my decision! I have already a sufficiently severe account to render to God, without charging my conscience with the addition of a new crime; and it would be an enormous one, to proscribe a religious Order, upon rumours and prejudices, or even upon suspicions. I shall not forget, that *in rendering to Cæsar the things that are Cæsar's, I ought to render to God the things that are God's.*

I have already ordered a person to examine the Archives of the *Propoganda*, and to procure for me the correspondence of my illustrious brother and predecessor Sextus Quintus with Philip II. Besides, I have required the heads of the accusation to be sent me, supported by such testimonies as cannot be rejected. I shall secretly become the Advocate of those whose ruin is required of me, that I may seek every means of justifying them within myself, before I pronounce.

The King of Portugal, as well as the Kings of France, Spain and Naples, are too religious to disapprove of my proceeding.

If Religion requires sacrifices, all the Church shall hear me, and——

I wish it had been the will of Providence that I had not been reserved for such calamitous

mitous times; for in whatever way I act, I shall make some malcontents, I shall occasion murmurs, and render myself odious to a number of people whose esteem and friendship I sincerely desire.

I compare myself to one of the Prophets whom God raised in the midst of tempests; or to a soldier, who by his rank is exposed to combat, though his views may be only to peace, but by the post he holds, finds himself obliged to act, whether he likes it or not.

All is in the hands of God; may he direct my pen, my tongue and my heart! I will submit to every thing, and I will do every thing that ought to be done, without dreading the consequences, &c.

LETTER CXXXI.

TO A MONK, ONE OF HIS FRIENDS.

IF you believe that I am happy, you are deceived. After having been agitated the whole day, I frequently wake in the middle of the night, and sigh after my Cloister,

Cloister, my Cell, and my books. I may likewise say, that I look upon your situation with envy. What encourages me is, that God himself has placed me in the Chair of St. Peter, to the great surprise of the whole world; and if I am destined to any important work, he will support me.

God knows, I would give every drop of my blood to have All pacified, that the whole world might return to their duty; that they who have given offence would reform, and that there might be neither division nor suppression.

I will not come to the last extremities, unless I am pressed by powerful motives; so that posterity at least may do me justice, in case the present age refuse it to me. It is not That, however, about which I am anxious, but the Eternity to which I am so near approaching, and which is a more formidable prospect to Popes than to any of the rest of the world.

I shall send you an answer to what you require. You know that I do not forget my friends, and that if I do not see them so frequently as formerly, it is because business and solicitude stand centries over me; they are at my gate, in my chamber, and in my heart.

Mention me to my old acquaintance: I think sometimes of the astonishment they must have been in at hearing of my elevation.

But more particularly tell him with whom I studied, that he did not prophesy well, when he told our companions that I should certainly finish my days in France. There is no appearance of that being ever realised, or I should be destined for something very extraordinary indeed.

I am always your affectionate

CLEMENT.

AT CASTLE-GANDOLPHO.

LETTER CXIV.

TO R. P. AIME DE LAMBALLE, GENERAL OF THE CAPUCHINS.

I AM sincerely obliged to you for the Prayers which you put up to Heaven for my preservation. I have doubly need of them, as an individual, and as Head of the Church. I share all your pains and troubles, being convinced that you suffer with a spirit of penitence, and in a manner agreeable to God.

If you remain long at Paris, as I am afraid you must on account of your indisposition, you will have an opportunity of seeing M. Doria, whom I love in the fulness of my heart, as a Prelate who will one day be the joy and honour of the Church. I see you in the midst of a world where there are great vices and great virtues; and where, by a particular Providence, the zeal for Religion so eminent in his Most Christian Majesty, and all the Royal Family, and the great piety of the Prelate who holds the See of Paris, bids fair to stop the progress of infidelity.

Bring with you some French Monk, whose knowledge will do honour here to his nation.

The Dominicans thought prudently when they called to the Minerva your worthy Countryman T. Fabrici, who will perpetuate

perpetuate the glory of the Order by his learning.

If your illness does not prevent you from going to see Madam Louise, I beg you will tell her how much I admire the sacrifice she has made. Assure all your Brotherhood that I love them sincerely in the Lord, and that I exhort them to live always in a manner worthy of our Founder.

I shall speak to Cardinal de Bernis upon what you desired me. You will have frequent inquiries made about him in France, for I know that he is as dear to the French as he is to the Italians.

I wish to see you again in good health, for I am intirely yours, as before,

(Signed)   CLEMENT XIV.

ROME, 2d April, 1773.

BULL,
BRIEFS,
DISCOURSES, &c.
OF
CLEMENT XIV.

CIRCULAR LETTER

OF

CLEMENT XIV.

TO ALL THE PATRIARCHS, PRI-
MATES, ARCHBISHOPS, AND BI-
SHOPS, ON THE SUBJECT OF THE
ADVANCEMENT

JESUS.

IN PERPETUAM REI MEMORIAM.

Dominus ac Redemptor.

QUI à ſupremâ hac Petri cathedrâ
...

CIRCULAR LETTER

OF

CLEMENT XIV.

TO ALL THE PATRIARCHS, PRIMATES, ARCHBISHOPS AND BISHOPS, ON THE SUBJECT OF HIS ADVANCEMENT.

CLEMENT XIV.

TO OUR VENERABLE BRETHREN, HEALTH AND APOSTOLICAL BENEDICTION.

BUT it is the work of the Lord, and it is wonderful in our eyes. The inscrutable Decrees of God, and not human councils, have loaded us with the awful duties of the Apostleship, when we were very far from entertaining any such thoughts. This conviction gives us full confidence, that He who hath called us to the painful cares of the supreme Ministry, will condescend to calm our fears, assist our weakness, and hear our Prayers. Peter, who ought to be

our

our model, was encouraged by the Lord, who reproached him for his want of faith when he thought he was sinking in the sea. There is no doubt but that it is the will of our Divine Chief, who in the person of the Prince of Apostles hath trusted to us the keys of the kingdom of Heaven, and hath commanded us to feed his sheep, that we put away all doubt of obtaining his aid. We submit ourselves then, without reserve, to Him, who is our strength and our help, resigning ourselves up to his power and truth. By his goodness he will complete in us the work which he hath begun; and even our lowliness will serve to make his mercy shine forth with more lustre in the eyes of men: for if, in these wretched times, he hath resolved to accomplish something for the good of his Church by the ministry of so useless a servant as we, all mankind will evidently see that he is the Author and Perfecter, and that to him alone the glory ought to be ascribed. But the more powerful the help is upon which we depend, the more ought we to employ our utmost efforts to co-operate with it; and

the

the more exalted the honour to which we have been advanced, the more ought we to endeavour worthily to difcharge the duties of it.

In proportion as we caft our eyes over all the countries of the Chriftian world, we perceive you, our venerable Brethren, fharing with us in our glorious work; and this view fills us with confolation. It is with the greateft joy we recognife in you, our worthy affiftants, faithful Paftors and evangelical labourers. It is therefore that we are anxious to addrefs ourfelves to you at the beginning of our Apoftlefhip. It is into your bofoms that we would fhed the moft fecret fentiments of our foul; and if it appears that we offer you fome exhortations, and give you fome advice, do not attribute it to any thing but diftruft of ourfelves, and think that they are the effects of that confidence which your virtues and filial love towards us have infpired.

Firft, we pray and befeech you, our venerable Brethren, to pray conftantly to God to ftrengthen our weaknefs; render us back

this

this return of the tenderneſs we bear towards you. Pray for our wants, as we pray for yours; ſo that being mutually ſuſtained, we may be more firm and more vigilant. Let us prove by the union of our hearts, that unity by which we all make only one and the ſame body; for the whole Church is but one building, of which the Prince of Apoſtles laid the foundation here. Many ſtones have been bound together for its conſtruction; but all reſt upon one alone, and he is Jeſus Chriſt, in whom we are all united as his members.

Being charged, as his Vicar, with the adminiſtration of his power, we are raiſed by his will to the moſt eminent ſituation; but united with us as the Chief of the viſible Church, you are the principal parts of that ſame body. Nothing can happen to the one, but muſt affect the other. Likewiſe, there is nothing that can intereſt you, but what muſt become an object of our ſolicitude. It is therefore, that being in perfect agreement, and animated with the ſame ſpirit, which flowing from the ſupreme

Head,

Head, and scattered over all the members, gives them life; we ought chiefly to labour that the whole body of the Church be sound and intire, and neither contract spot or wrinkle, but flourish by the practice of every Christian virtue. With the Divine help we may succeed in this, if every one, according to his power, would inflame himself with zeal in the care of the flock which is entrusted to him, and apply carefully to guard them from seduction, to procure them solid instructions, and the proper means of sanctification.

There never was a time when it was more necessary to watch for the safety of souls. Opinions are every day scattered abroad, most capable of shaking the cause of Religion; and men in crouds allow themselves to be seduced by a thirst after novelty. It is a mortal poison, which insinuates itself into all conditions, and which makes the most cruel ravages.

My Reverend Brethren, it is a new motive for our labouring with more ardour than ever, to repress a madness which dares to attack the moſt holy Laws, and even to inſult the Deity.

It is not by the help of human wiſdom that you will ſucceed in this pious enterprise, but by the ſimplicity of the word of God, more piercing than a two-edged ſword. You will eaſily repel all the attacks of the enemy, you will eaſily blunt all their arrows, by preſenting in all your diſcourſes only Jeſus Chriſt, and Jeſus Chriſt crucified. He hath built his Church, that Holy City, and provided it with his Laws and his Precepts. He hath truſted to it the Faith which he came to eſtabliſh, as a depoſit to be religiouſly preſerved in all its purity. It was his will that it ſhould become the impregnable rampart of his Doctrine and Truth, and that the gates of hell ſhould never prevail againſt it. Being appointed to the care and government of this Holy City, our venerable Brethren, let us diligently preſerve the precious inheritance of the Faith of our Holy Founder and Divine Maſter, which our Fathers have tranſmitted to us in all its purity, that we may tranſmit it equally pure to our deſcendants. If our actions

actions and counsels are conformable to the rule marked out for us in the Holy Scriptures, if we walk in the paths of our Fathers which cannot lead us astray, we may assure ourselves that we shall be able to shun every false step which is capable of weakening the Faith of the Christian people, or in any point injure the unity of the Church. Let us only draw from the Scriptures, and from tradition, what it imports us to know and to observe; these are the sacred sources of Divine Wisdom; and there we shall find whatever we ought to believe and practise; whatever concerns worship, discipline, or manner of living, is included in that double deposit. We shall there see the depth of our sublime Mysteries, the duties of Piety, the rules of Justice and Humanity. There we shall be instructed in what we owe to God, to the Church, to our country, and to our neighbour; and we must acknowledge that there is no law better than true Religion, to establish the rights of nations and society. The Doctrines of Jesus Christ have never been attacked without troubling the repose of the people, without disturbing the obedience due to Sovereigns, and without scattering troubles and confusion all around.

There is such an intimate union between the rights of his Divine Majesty, and the rights of the Kings of this world, that when the laws of Christianity are observed, Sovereigns are obeyed without regret, their power is respected, and their persons honoured.

We therefore exhort you, our venerable Brethren, to inculcate, to the utmost of your power, obedience and submission to Sovereigns in the people that are intrusted to you; for among the Commandments of God, this is extremely necessary for preserving peace and good order. Kings have been elevated to the eminent ranks they possess, only to watch over the safety of the public, and to confine men within the bounds of wisdom and equity. They are the Ministers of God for the observance of justice, and they only carry the sword to execute the vengeance of God, by punishing those that stray from their duty. They

are

are likewise the dear Children and the Protectors of the Church, and it is their duty to defend her rights, and support her interests. Take care then, that you instruct even the children, as soon as they are capable of it, to preserve an inviolable fidelity towards their Sovereigns, to submit to their authority, to observe their laws, not only from the fear of punishment, but as a duty of conscience.

When by your zeal and application you shall have thus disposed the minds of subjects to obey their Kings, to respect and love them in the fullness of their hearts, you will then have laboured effectually for the tranquillity of the people, and the good of the Church; for the one is inseparable from the other. But that you may infallibly acquit yourselves with success in that duty, you should join to the Prayers which you daily make for the people, particular Prayers for the Kings, so as to obtain from God their preservation and prosperity, and the grace which is necessary to govern with wisdom and with equity.

Thus

Thus, in labouring for the happiness of all mankind, you will worthily discharge the duties of your sacred Ministry; for it is just and right that the Pontiffs, who have been established for the good of man, in what concerns the worship of God, should present to God the vows of all the faithful, incessantly praying the Lord to support and establish him who watcheth for the public tranquillity, and the preservation of all the people.

It would be superfluous to remind you of all the other obligations which the pastoral dignity imposes on you. You are already fully instructed in all the duties which the Christian Religion requires, living happily in the practice of all the virtues: for you should never fail to have Jesus Christ our Chief, the Prince of all Pastors, before your eyes, and still endeavour to render yourselves as near a copy as possible of that perfect model of Charity, Holiness, and Humility. Our labours, our thoughts, cannot have a more glorious or more excellent object than Him, who being the brightness

ness of his Father's glory, and the express image of his person, has been pleased to raise us to the quality of Children of God, by adoption, and to make us co-heirs with himself. It is the way to preserve the union and alliance of men with Jesus Christ, and to imitate that Divine Model of patience, gentleness, and humility. Wherefore it is said: *Ascend upon a high mountain, ye who preach the Gospel to Sion.*

If you have an ardent desire to conform to these duties, it is not possible but this holy ardour must by sympathy communicate itself from your heart to the breasts of all nations, and they become deeply inflamed with it; for the example of the Pastor has a virtue and astonishing power in moving the souls of the Faithful intrusted to his charge. When they perceive that all his thoughts and all his actions are regulated by the model of all perfection; when they see him avoid every thing which can relish of austerity, fierceness, and haughtiness; and employ himself only in works which inspire charity, gentleness, and humility;

humility; then will they find themselves animated to follow such an admirable and edifying example.

When they are convinced that a Pastor neglects himself to be useful to others; that his principal delight is to relieve the indigent; that he comforts the afflicted, instructs the ignorant, assists with his good offices and his counsels all those who stand in need of them; and that, in fine, every thing bespeaks a perfect disposition in him to sacrifice his life for the salvation of his people; then every one, struck with his virtues, and affected by his example, will enter into himself, and correct his faults. But if a Pastor, attached solely to his own interest, prefers the things of this world to those of Heaven, how can he engage his flock to love God only, and to render services to each other? If he sighs after riches, pleasures, and honours, how can he inspire the contempt of them? If he is haughty, and blown up with pride, how will he persuade them to be gentle and humble?

Since

Since then you are charged, our venerable Brethren, to form the people according to the maxims of Jesus Christ, your first duty is to live in the holiness, gentleness, and innocence of manners, of which he hath set us an example. You may depend upon it, you cannot make a proper use of your authority, but by endeavouring rather to give proofs of your modesty and charity, than by displaying the badges of your dignity. Be assured, that if you acquit yourselves scrupulously of the duties imposed upon you, you will be crowned with glory and happiness; and that, on the contrary, if you neglect them, you will be covered with shame, and prepare for yourselves the greatest of all miseries. Do not desire other riches than to secure those souls to God, which he hath purchased with his blood:—seek no other glory than that of consecrating yourselves intirely to the Lord, to labour incessantly in extending his worship, to set off the beauty of his House, to extirpate vice, and cultivate virtue. Such should be the sole object of your

your thoughts, your defires, your actions, and your ambition. And do not think, our venerable Brethren, that after having paſſed a long time in theſe painful labours, there will remain nothing more to exerciſe your virtue. Such is the nature of our Miniſtry, ſuch is the condition of a Biſhop, that he ought never to ſee an end to his ſolicitude and cares; he can never give himſelf up to reſt; for they whoſe charity ſhould know no bounds, ought to admit no bounds to their activity. The expectation of an eternal reward, is ſurely capable of rendering all our labour light.

Ah! what can appear difficult to thoſe who do not loſe ſight of the ineffable happineſs which the Lord will ſhare with all thoſe who faithfully watch and increaſe his flock, when he comes to aſk an account of their adminiſtration! Beſide this hope, ſo ſweet and precious, you will find inexpreſſible joy and conſolation in the very labours of an Epiſcopal life. When God Almighty ſeconds our efforts, we ſee the people ſtrictly united by the ties of reciprocal

procal charity, and diftinguifhing themfelves by their innocence, candour, and piety: we fee a multitude of excellent fruits, which our watchings, fatigue, and cares, have produced in the fields of the Church.

May we, our moft dear and venerable Brethren, by our unanimous and voluntary agreement, zeal, and application, revive in the time of our Apoftlefhip that flourifhing ftate of Religion, and reftore all the beauty it poffeffed in the firft ages! May we be able to congratulate, and rejoice with, you in the Lord! May the God of mercy deign to fupport us by the help of his grace, and fill our hearts with whatever is agreeable to him!

In teftimony of our charity, We give you, with all poffible affection, and all the Faithful of your Churches, the Apoftolical Benediction.

<small>At ROME, St. MARY MAJOR, the 12th of December, in the Year 1769, and the Firft of our Pontificate.</small>

LETTER.

To His Most CHRISTIAN MAJESTY, LOUIS XV.

UPON IRRELIGION.

WE know nothing more proper to kindle your zeal, than the motive which engages us to write to you. We do not purpose to speak at present of our personal interests, but those of Religion itself. If we are assured of your royal protection for ourselves, we have much more reason to believe that you will not reject our solicitations, which have no other view than the good of the Church.

It is the common cause of God and Christianity, which we at present speak of to you, our most dear Son in Jesus Christ. We see with the deepest sorrow, the worship established by the Supreme Legislator, for a long time attacked by wicked men, who do not cease to direct against it the sacrilegious arrows of their perverse spirits. It may be said, that there is a general conspiracy, by the most audacious efforts, utterly to overthrow whatever is most venerable

venerable or sacred. They do not blush to produce every day a croud of writings, an eternal monument of their folly, in order to destroy even the first principles of good morals, to break the bonds of all Society, and to seduce simple souls, by the fatal talent which they possess of successfully sowing these perverse doctrines.

The astonishing rapidity of their progress persuades us, that there can be nothing more important, or more urgent, than to raise a dyke to oppose this torrent.

It is not sufficient to take all the poisoned works which issue from that horrid School, out of the hands of Readers; the zeal of our venerable Brethren the Bishops must come to our assistance; that by uniting our strength, we may, with one common accord, combat the different enemies of our Religion, and be avenged of the insults daily offered to it.

We see with inexpressible joy upon this occasion, that the Prelates of Your Majesty's great and flourishing Empire, at present assembled in Paris for the affairs of the Clergy, enter perfectly into our views,

views, and that their paftoral folicitude engages them to employ every means of ftopping the ravages of infidelity. We have a perfect confidence that in labouring, as they will do, in the caufe of God, they will receive abundantly the fpirit of wifdom and ftrength. It is no fmall confolation to us, to fee them apply with fo much zeal to the difcharge of fuch important duties.

But if they have need of the protection of the Moft High, they have likewife a right to expect from you, our moft dear Son, the neceffary helps to affift and crown their labours. We therefore pray you, as much as in us lies, to favour them in whatever they do for the caufe of Religion, and to fupport them with vigour. Then will they give effectual proofs of the zeal which animates them, not only for the falvation of the Faithful, but for the temporal advantage of their Country, and alfo for your facred Perfon; for Religion being the firmeft fupport of Thrones, it is eafy to retain people who obey God, in obedience to Kings.

From

Hence it is eafy to be feen, that our cares and folicitude do not tend lefs to confirm your royal authority, than to maintain the interefts of God. Human focieties are much more indebted for their prefervation and fecurity to the exercife of the true worfhip, and the ftability of the revealed doctrine, than to the force of arms, or the abundance of riches.

The true way of drawing down the moft precious effects of the Divine mercy upon your facred Perfon, and upon the Princes and Princeffes of your blood, is publicly to maintain the Faith and Piety in their purity. In doing this you will eminently poffefs the art of reigning, the art by which your anceftors have always fhewn themfelves Moft Chriftian Kings; and you will fupport your own glory and theirs, by adding the moft ftriking proofs of your Religion to their example.

This fubject would no doubt require to be treated more fully; but the high opinion we have of your truly royal piety, makes us look upon a long Difcourfe on this fubject as fuperfluous.

, In the firm perfuafion that Your Majefty will grant what we afk with equal zeal and juftice, we pray the Almighty, by whom you reign, that he will long preferve you and your Auguft Family; and we give you, with all poffible tendernefs, our Apoftolical Benediction. May it be a happy prefage of the favour and happinefs which we wifh you!

ROME, 21ft March, 1770.

To MADAME LOUISE OF FRANCE,
CLEMENT XIV.

TO OUR MOST DEAR DAUGHTER IN JESUS CHRIST, ALL HEALTH!

IT feemeth to us that the moft painful labours of the Apoftlefhip with which we have been clothed, have no longer any thing but what is light and pleafing, fince we have learnt your holy and generous refolution. You could undertake nothing more grand nor more fublime, than to exchange the pomp of a Royal Court for the humiliation of a Religious Houfe.

Whether

Whether we confider the pious condefcenfion of our moft dear Son in Jefus Chrift, Louis, your Auguft Father, and Moft Chriftian King, who has permitted you to make fuch a facrifice; or look upon the precious advantage which muft thence refult for the good of the Church; we cannot contain our joy and admiration.

May thanks be rendered to God, the Author of all good, that he has given us, in your perfon, fuch a ftriking example to all Princes, and all Nations, and has deigned to confecrate our Pontificate by fo glorious an event. It is a fubject of congratulation for us, as well as for you. Ah! how can we be otherwife than delighted with the view of the abundant riches which the Lord hath heaped upon you; and with that all-divine ftrength which made you, after the moft mature reflexions, embrace a kind of life which may be called a fketch of Heaven! None but God himfelf could infpire you with fuch a generous defign. You have learnt, by the favour of his light, that all the grandeurs of this world are only vapours; all its pleafures, mere illufions;

all its promises, arrant falsehoods; and lastly, that the soul can only find peace in the pleasing exercise of the love of God; and that you cannot reign, but by serving him alone.

Now it is, that, in the port where you are at present, sheltered from rocks and shipwreck, you are about to enjoy the most delicious tranquillity; to taste, more than ever, the holy and divine pleasures which are the inheritance of the friends of God. When we can triumph over the world, we possess the greatest riches, in the midst of indigence. We find true liberty in renouncing ourselves; grandeur and glory in the depressions of the profoundest humility. Nothing is comparable to the happiness of concentrating all our thoughts, and all our desires, in the bosom of God; to live with Him alone, to be inflamed with the love of Him, and to have no other hope but that of possessing Him forever.

May your courage increase, our most dear Daughter, in proportion as the grace of God has been plentifully poured upon you! Persevere, with all your strength,

in

in the noble defign which you have formed, of proceeding in the way of Salvation. Employ yourfelf conftantly with Him, whom you have propofed to love and ferve all the days of your life: think that the recompence which is the object of your defires, is infinite; and the fruit which you expect, incorruptible: By that means you will change your toils into delights, and you will tafte beforehand the fweets of a heaven to come.

The more we reflect upon the generous ftep which you have taken, the more we rejoice in the hope, that the brilliant example will produce in many other people the defire of imitating it. You will not fail to call to mind that the King, your indulgent Father, having facrificed the pleafure he had in your fociety that he might not oppofe your call, you ought to employ every means of teftifying your gratitude towards him. The only way to acquit yourfelf is, to pray continually to God, to make him happy in this life, and in that which is to come.

Your

Your zeal for the Church, which is well known to us, together with your respectful attachment to the Holy See, are new motives of joy and consolation; for we are persuaded that you will apply constantly to God for our particular wants, as well as those of Religion. We offer you in acknowledgement of all these good offices, every advantage which you can expect from our paternal tenderness. Nothing can equal the extreme desire which we have to second your pious intentions, and to promote the fervour with which you walk in the paths of virtue. And although we are perfectly convinced of your zeal and perseverance, we will willingly give to your present or future Confessor the power of softening your Rule, and even to dispense with it in every case where your weakness cannot keep pace with your courage. Besides that, we grant you, in virtue of our Apostolical authority, a full and intire indulgence every time you approach the Holy Table; and to testify our affection still more, we grant the same favour to our Holy Daughters in Jesus Christ,

Chrift, your worthy Companions, and make them participators with you in our Apoftolical Benediction.

Given at ROME, 9th May, 1770, the firft Year of our Pontificate.

LETTER

To His Moft CHRISTIAN MAJESTY, LOUIS XV.

ON THE SUBJECT OF MADAME LOUISE TAKING THE HABIT.

OUR MOST DEAR SON IN JESUS CHRIST, ALL HEALTH!

IT is proper that at the fame time we write to our moft dear Daughter in Jefus Chrift, the Princefs Louifa Maria, to congratulate her on the greatnefs of her facrifice, we pour forth our joy into the paternal bofom of your Majefty. You have given us the greateft delight; and the more fo, as you have had the principal fhare in fo remarkable and fo fplendid an action. But what fills our Soul with infinite fatisfaction, is, that after having applauded the generous proceeding of your

Auguft

August Daughter, you have shewn extraordinary courage, in separating yourself from her, notwithstanding the inestimable qualities which rendered her so dear to you; and that as soon as you believed you heard the voice of Religion, you stifled the call of Nature, and have only seen a future Spouse for Jesus Christ, in her who was your beloved Daughter. Thus you yourself have opened the way to Heaven to a pious Princess who desired with ardour to enter it; and you have contributed, by your generous approbation, to secure her from the dangers which surround human life, and the tumultuous waves which distract it.

I see her in the holy retreat which she hath chosen, teaching the whole world that there is nothing more frail, nor more vain, than all the delights and all the grandeur of this life; that they are to be looked upon only as rocks, which often become the lamentable cause of a multitude of evils, by opposing the acquisition of eternal happiness.

The

The share which you have had in so pious an action, ought to give you the greatest confidence in the prayers of your illustrious Daughter: she will never cease to pray to God for your August Person, your Royal Family and your whole Kingdom, and, what should still more interest your Majesty, for the salvation of your soul. It is a powerful intercession which you have obtained in the sight of the Almighty; and it much concerns you to derive every possible advantage from an event which Providence has permitted for your good.

We wish, in the fulness of our heart, that you would receive the testimonies of our affection, as the tender overflowings of the heart of a Father who dearly loves you, and who is no less zealous for your glory and happiness than his own. To convince you of it, we give you, our most dear Son in Jesus Christ, in the most affectionate manner possible, our Apostolical Benediction, as an undoubted proof of the singular love that, &c.

Given at ROME, 9th May, 1770, and the First of our Pontificate.

A SECOND LETTER

To His Most CHRISTIAN MAJESTY,

LOUIS XV.

ON THE SAME SUBJECT.

AFTER having congratulated Your Majesty, by our Letter of the 9th of May last, on the heroic courage with which the Princess Louisa, your August Daughter, is about to embrace a religious life; after having testified the fulness of our joy on the same subject to her; we cannot resist expressing our satisfaction again this day, and what our transports are at the approach of such a sacrifice. Her zeal is so ardent, that she can suffer no longer delay, and she is inflamed with the desire of seeing herself clothed in the Holy Habit of the Carmelites, by the hands of our Venerable Brother, Bernardin, Archbishop of Damascus, our Nuncio in Ordinary to Your Majesty.

From

From the first news we received of her generous design, we recognised the spirit of God acting in a most wonderful manner on the soul of this August Princess; and we found ourselves affected with the strongest desire to go in person to perform the ceremony of the *Vesture*, which our Nuncio is to perform, and thereby augment the lustre and solemnity of so great a day. But the distance making it impossible, we shall accomplish our desires in part, by charging our Nuncio, our Brother abovenamed, with this august duty. We will seem to assist in some sort ourselves, and lead our most dear daughter in Jesus Christ to the nuptials of her Divine Spouse. We pray you to approve of the Letters which we have addressed on that subject to the Nuncio who represents us; and we persuade ourselves that you will acquiesce the more willingly, as these dispositions have no other motive than our zeal and affection for your Majesty.

As a certain pledge of these sentiments, and as a happy presage of the
divine

divine blessing, receive our Apostolical Benediction. We give it with all the tenderness of a Father to you, and to all your August Children, especially the pious Princess who is the memorable subject of our gladness.

> Given at ROME, the 18th of July, 1770, the second Year of our Pontificate.

SECOND LETTER

TO MADAM LOUISE, OF FRANCE.

OUR MOST DEAR DAUGHTER IN JESUS CHRIST, ALL HEALTH!

AT last the most glorious and the most fortunate day of your life approaches; a day on which, by the most sacred and intimate ties, you are to become the Spouse of Jesus Christ himself; and devote to him all your desires, all your thoughts, and all your actions.

We were transported with joy, and we applauded your magnanimity, from that moment, when, treading the vanities of the world under your feet, you renounced the delights of the most brilliant Court, to confine

confine yourself to the obscurity of the Cloister, and there to make trial of the most humble and most mortifying life: but your public profession, by which you are about to make Heaven and earth witnesses of your generous sacrifice, completes our joy. Never forget that the Lord, by calling you from the bosom of grandeur to live under the shadow of the Cross, marked you with the Seal of Predestination. The higher the rank you held in the world, the more is his goodness remarkable, and the more ought your soul to be penetrated with love and gratitude.

All the festivals of this age have nothing to compare with that great day, when, led by the inspiration of Grace, you shall give yourself up intirely to God, and solemnly take him for your inheritance.

Would to Heaven, our dearest Daughter, that it were possible for us to assist in person at this august ceremony, to be not only a witness, but likewise the Minister of such an heroic sacrifice! Nevertheless,
although

although that happiness is denied us, we will not fail to enjoy it as much as possible, by having ourselves represented by our venerable Brother, the Archbishop of Damascus, our Nuncio in ordinary. It was already by his hands that we clothed you in the sacred habit, and it will be by him that we shall receive your sacred vows; and that nothing may be wanting for the solemnity of so great a day, we charge him to impart to you all the treasures of the Church.

We do not doubt of your shewing every sense of our paternal tenderness, by advancing more and more in the course you have entered, and by the constant practice of all the virtues, more especially that of humility. It is from thence you will learn that you cannot be vain of any thing, but that you hold all from God; that you ought constantly to distrust your own strength, and not rely on your own merit, but on his Almighty Grace only; believing, at the same time, that you are capable of every thing in Him who strengthens you,

and

and never ceasing to have recourse to his infinite mercy.

These sentiments, deeply engraved on your soul, will diffuse a Christian modesty over your whole person; and in the shadow of that humility, Divine Love will take root in your heart, and will produce fruit both useful and abundant.

It is not by way of advice that we speak to you in this manner, as if we thought you had need of it, but to render the way of life to which God hath called you, more precious.

You will certainly make it a capital duty to testify, upon all occasions, the lively gratitude which you owe to your August Father, who has loved you so tenderly, and done every thing for you: you will never cease to pray to God to preserve him, to prosper his kingdom and his august Family, and, above all, to grant him eternal happiness.

As for us, if we may be permitted to claim the rights which our affection intitles us to, we conjure you to draw down upon

our

our perſon, as your Father in Jeſus Chriſt, the favourable attention of the Lord, and to pray continually for theChurch intruſted to our care. And now that you are more intimately attached to her, you ought to intereſt yourſelf more than ever in what concerns either her advantage or glory. On your part, you may be perſuaded that we will continually beg of God to bleſs your pious reſolutions, and that you may increaſe more and more in his holy love.

Receive, as a pledge of our paternal affection, our Apoſtolical Benediction; we give it you with all our heart, and likewiſe to all the Order of Carmelites, with whom you are about to be aſſociated for ever.

· Given at ROME, at St. MARY-MAJOR, under the FISHERMAN'S-RING, the 14th of Auguſt, 1771, and the third Year of our Pontificate.

LETTER

LETTER

TO MONSIGNOR GIRAULT, ARCHBISHOP OF DAMASCUS, NUNCIO TO HIS MOST CHRISTIAN MAJESTY.

To our venerable Brother, Health and Apostolical Benediction!

HAVING learned that the Princess Louise-Marie of France, our most dear Daughter in Jesus Christ, retired to the Monastery of the Bare-footed Carmelites of St. Denis, desires with the most lively ardour to embrace their holy institution, in order to satisfy her devotion, she ought to receive the habit at your hands, as being Superior of the Order.

When I think of that Princess, born in the midst of the delights and grandeur of the most brilliant Court in the world, devoting herself to the most austere and retired life, I cannot help admiring, and at the same time acknowledging the impression of the Holy Ghost, so as to say, 'It is a miracle of the Most High.' We are so deeply

deeply penetrated on this occasion, that to accord with the inexpressible sentiments of the zeal with which we are animated, and the joy which transports us, we charge you to perform this ceremony in our name.

Thus then, to give to this holy and celebrated Office all the lustre which it merits, and all the solemnity of which it is susceptible, we specially depute you, our venerable Brother, and delegate you to act for us in our place.

This interests us the more deeply, as we shall believe we are there present, to see with our own eyes with what holy transports our most dear Daughter in Jesus Christ will unite herself, with all her heart, to her heavenly Husband.

Besides this, as we are desirous to augment the general satisfaction of the Order, and to render it more complete, by giving to all those who compose it the spiritual treasures of the Church; by the effect of our good-will, we grant plenary indulgence to all the Bare-footed Carmelites of the kingdom of France, who, on the day of

the

the Princefs taking the habit, fhall partake of the Sacraments of Penitence and the Eucharift, and implore the mercy of the Almighty for the exaltation of the Holy Catholic Church, for our moſt dear ſon in Jeſus Chriſt Louis Moſt Chriſtian King of France, for his Children, for the Royal Family, and particularly for the Princefs who is at preſent the ſubject of our joy, and who is to begin her Noviciate in the moſt auſtere and ſacred ſtate; that new grace may be heaped upon her from day to day; that ſhe may become more the ornament of her Order by the regularity of her life, than by the ſplendor of her name.—And you, our venerable Brother, we deſire you diligently to inform all whom it may concern, of the ſalutary favour with which we are willing to gratify them: and for a proof of our Pontifical good-will, we give you, &c.

ROME, 18 July, 1770, the ſecond Year
of our Pontificate.

LETTER

TO HIS MOST CHRISTIAN MAJESTY.

OUR MOST DEAR SON IN JESUS CHRIST, ALL HEALTH!

EVERY time we think of your illustrious Daughter, Louife-Marie of France, who in Jefus Chrift is likewife ours, we blefs God that he hath fo infpired her.—We have conftantly before our eyes the great example which fhe fets to the world; an example which will do honour to this age, and will be the admiration of pofterity. The nearer the moment of the facrifice approaches, the more we redouble our prayers, and the more we defire to declare to you the fentiments which attach us to your perfon, by rendering the tribute of praife which is due to you for the part you have taken in this great event, of which the Church is to be the witnefs.

Undoubtedly you could not do better than fecure to yourfelf a fupport in the prayers and vows of her who is totally devoted to

your

your perſon, and is intirely agreeable to
God. In this your wiſdom is as eminent
as your Religion; and it is that which per-
ſuades us, at the ſame time, that the Divine goodneſs will make you reap the
greateſt advantage from ſo favourable an
event. We congratulate you with all our
heart, and applaud ourſelves, becauſe the
union with our moſt dear Daughter in Jeſus
Chriſt will become more ſtrong than ever.
Our greateſt deſire would be to tie theſe
knots ſtill more cloſe, by preſiding at the
ceremony which we ſee approaching, and
receiving in perſon the moſt ſolemn vows
which the moſt tender piety can pronounce.

We are the more penetrated with this
thought, as it would be a moſt happy occa-
ſion of converſing with you, of embracing
you, and ſhewing you in our eyes, and on
our countenance, the ſentiments with which
you inſpire us. Then our paternal tenderneſs and our paſtoral charity ſhining forth,
would aſſure you in the ſtrongeſt manner
of our intire affection. But alas! we are

so unfortunately situated, as to have that satisfaction only in idea.

As to any other advantages, we have endeavoured to procure them, notwithstanding our absence; having chosen our venerable Brother the Archbishop of Damascus to supply our place, and given him the most special and extensive powers for that purpose, as we before did, when we gave him commission to represent us at the ceremony of taking the Habit.

Being informed that your Majesty then approved of the manner in which we had disposed these things for the ceremony of giving the Habit to our August Princess, we flatter ourselves that you will equally approve at present of the same dispositions.

We earnestly pray you, then, to join in our views with your usual goodness, and afford us the consolation to see our place supplied by him that represents us.

Receive, as the best proof which we can give of our attachment; our Apostolical Benediction, which, as a pledge of all the benedictions of Heaven, shall extend to
your

your auguſt race, and over your whole kingdom, if our prayers are heard.

Given at ROME, at St. MARIE-MAJOR's, under the FISHERMAN's-RING, the 14th of Auguſt, 1771, the third Year of our Pontificate.

LETTER

TO THE DUKE OF PARMA.

IT would be very difficult to expreſs all the ſatisfaction which your Letter gave us, in which we find ſentiments of the moſt tender affection. We are the more happy at preſent to receive ſuch marks of your friendſhip, as we have always been moſt ſingularly attached to you, and have never ceaſed to intereſt ourſelves in whatever could concern you.

We congratulate ourſelves, at the ſame time, on your having received with all poſſible good-will the teſtimonies of our friendſhip, (on account of the illuſtrious offspring that will one day be the heir of your virtues) and the proof of our acknowledgements for the zeal with which you laboured

boured for our reconciliation with his Moſt Chriſtian Majeſty. By it you have compleated the proofs of your piety towards the Holy See, and have taken a ſtep equally glorious and meritorious. The mediation which you have employed with our dear Sons in Jeſus Chriſt, the moſt virtuous Kings your Grandfather, Uncle, and Couſin, to engage them to eraſe from their minds every trace of old miſunderſtandings, and to reſtore to us the domains of Avignon, Benevento, and Porto Corvo, cannot fail to be moſt effectual. You do us juſtice in being convinced of our extreme love for peace and concord, particularly with the auguſt Houſe of Bourbon, which has always deſerved ſo well from us, from the Chair of St. Peter, and the whole Church in general.—We never doubted that the Religion and wiſdom of theſe Sovereigns would inſpire them with the ſame pacific ſentiments which we cheriſh in our own breaſt. We conceive the ſtrongeſt hopes from your mediation, becauſe of your royal virtues, and the love which your auguſt relations muſt reaſonably have for you.

you. They will join with more zeal to second your good intentions, when they see peace and harmony restored from the same source from whence the misunderstanding and disagreement had proceeded. In return, we will seize every opportunity of proving to you, in the most distinguished manner, our gratitude and affection.

We give you, with all the tenderness of a paternal affection, our Apostolical Benediction, as likewise to your virtuous Spouse, and to your dear new-born Son; and we pray the Almighty God that you may increase in virtue from day to day, and acquire that glory which he hath reserved for the Elect.

SECOND LETTER

TO THE DUKE OF PARMA.

AS soon as we were informed of the pains you had taken to reconcile us with the Kings our most dear Sons in Jesus Christ, and restore to the Holy See its ancient possessions, we resolved to render you our most sincere thanks. Now that your wisdom has compleated this great work, we must publicly proclaim our joy and gratitude. We assure you that we will never forget this generous proceeding, which has procured us such signal advantages; and that the paternal tenderness which we have for you, is equal to your great virtues. We therefore pray, in the fulness of our heart, for whatever can contribute to your glory and happiness. The Marquis de Lano, to whom we are tenderly attached, on account of his merit and services to us, has doubtless declared to you what our sentiments are with regard to you. It is to cement them more and more, that we
continually

continually pray to God to second, by the abundance of his heavenly gifts, the Apostolical Benediction with which we salute you as the most certain pledge of our affection, &c.

BRIEF.

To our dear Son PETER FRANCIS BOUDIER, at present SUPERIOR-GENERAL of BENEDICTINES, of the CONGREGATION of St. MAUR, and GRAND-PRIOR of the ROYAL ABBEY of St. DENIS,

CLEMENT XIV.

To our dear Son, Health and Apostolical Benediction!

YOUR Letter, dictated by respect, attachment, and most tender love, evidently proves the joy which you and your Congregation felt upon our elevation to the Sovereign Pontificate. Your sentiments for the Apostolical Chair were already known to us, and the new testimonies which you give us of them, were not wanted

wanted to perfuade us of your attachment to the Holy See.

We have likewife been very fenfible of the demonftrations of zeal, to which you and your Congregation have added a new value, in begging the Father of Mercies to fupport and fortify our weaknefs, by his powerful help, in the adminiftration of fuch an important employment.

As to the judgement which you have formed of Us, We fee nothing but your indulgence, your filial love, and the ardent zeal with which you are animated for Us. On Our part, We exceedingly defire to have fome opportunity of teftifying all the good-will we bear towards you, and thofe who are fubmitted to your care. In the mean time, as a pledge of our paternal tendernefs, We give to you, Our dear Son, and to your Brethren, with the fulleft effufion of Our heart, Our Apoftolical Benediction.

<small>Given at ROME, at St. MARIE-MAJOR, under the FISHERMAN's RING, the 11th Auguft, 1769, and the firft of our Pontificate.</small>

BENEDICT STAY.

BRIEF

To our dear Son BODDAERT, PRIOR-GENERAL of the Order of GUILLELMITES.

CLEMENT XIV.

To our dear Son, health and Apostolical Benediction!

THE joy which you testify at Our advancement to the Sovereign Pontificate, agrees with the attachment which your Order has a long time had for us. We do not doubt of your adding to those exterior proofs of your zeal, the assistance of your prayers to God that he will deign to help our weakness; and therefore we at present beg the continuance of them, as the effect of your charity for us. As to our sentiments with regard to you, the instances which we have formerly given of our good-will towards you, sufficiently shew what you may expect. Be assured that our new dignity, far from lessening that good-will, has rather increased it; especially after the testimony you have given us, that having carefully visited the Monasteries of your Order, you have found them

them obedient to the Rules of their Institution. This assurance on your part has given us the greatest pleasure;—it redoubles the tenderness which we have for you; and to give you a pledge of it, we grant to you, our dear Son, and to all the Order intrusted to your care, with all the effusion of our heart, Our Apostolical Benediction.

> Given at ROME, at St. MARY-MAJOR, under the Fisherman's Ring, the 9th of July, 1769. and the First of our Pontificate.
>
> BENEDICT STAY.

SPEECH

SPOKEN BY CLEMENT XIV. IN THE SECRET CONSISTORY HELD THE 21st SEPTEMBER, 1770;

ON THE SUBJECT OF THE RECONCILIATION OF PORTUGAL WITH THE COURT OF ROME.

IT seems, Our venerable Brethren, that Providence hath chosen this day, the twenty-fourth of the month, for me to notify to you the great event on account of which we are assembled in this place; the anniversary of my arrival in Rome; of my advancement to the Purple, however unworthy of the honour; and lastly, the day on which I am to announce to you a full and entire reconciliation with the Court of Portugal.

We have juſt received the moſt ſincere and the moſt eminent proofs of the ſubmiſſion and zeal of his Moſt Faithful Majeſty:—they have even ſurpaſſed our expectation. Not only the ſame old cuſtoms and attachment which had ever before ſubſiſted between us and that Crown are now again renewed, but likewiſe confirmed in ſuch a manner that they have acquired new ſtrength.

When we foretold what has juſt now happened, we founded our hopes upon the faith and piety of our moſt dear Son in Jeſus Chriſt, who at all times gave the moſt unqueſtionable proofs of his zeal for the true religion. The day we were informed of his reconciliation, increaſed the glory and advantage of the Holy See, by filling us with conſolation and joy. There is, therefore, nothing which we ought not to undertake to teſtify our acknowledgements to his Moſt Faithful Majeſty, and no wiſh which we ought not to form for

his

his prefervation, and that of Marie-Anne-Victoire, his auguft and dear Spoufe, who rivalled him in her great zeal to bring about this accommodation. The Count d'Oyeras, Secretary of State, is equally deferving of our gratitude and praife; and we fhould not forget the Governor of Almada, Minifter Plenipotentiary with Us; and whom we have often heard, with the greateft joy, declare to us the pious and laudable fentiments of his Moft Faithful Majefty. As there is no method more proper to acquit ourfelves of our gratitude to a Prince fo deferving of praife, than to pray God to profper him; let us beg of him continually to grant us that great favour, &c.

SPEECH

SPEECH

OF

CLEMENT XIV. IN THE SECRET CONSISTORY, HELD THE 6th JUNE, 1774.

UPON THE DEATH OF LOUIS XV.

VENERABLE BRETHREN,

IF any thing could confole us in the midſt of our painful labours, it is to know that Louis, the Moſt Chriſtian King, had the beſt intentions and the greateſt attachment to religion, as likewiſe to our perſon; but alas! that confolation becomes at this day the ſubject of the deepeſt ſorrow. Our life has been a ſtate of affliction ever ſince we heard of his death; an event truly fatal, and the conſequence of a muſt cruel diſorder. We are the more deeply affected, as we have loſt him in that moment, when he had juſt given us the moſt conſpicuous proofs of his juſtice, magnanimity, and tender affection towards us and the Holy Apoſtolical See. And what afflicts us yet more, is, that we cannot now acquit ourſelves to-

wards

wards him, but by our tears and our regret.

Nevertheless, let us adore the decrees of Divine Providence; and in submitting to the will of the Almighty, upon whom the fate of Kings absolutely depends, let us acknowledge that all is directed by his wisdom, and for his glory.

Nothing but this resignation to the Divine will can lessen our sorrow. We no sooner learned the danger with which the King's life was threatened, than we addressed our most fervent prayers to Heaven, to obtain his recovery. All France united their supplications with ours, and all the Royal Family, shedding torrents of tears, acquitted themselves of the same duty; particularly our most dear Daughter in Jesus Christ, Marie-Louise of France, who from her holy retreat raised her pious hands towards Heaven, and gave vent to the deepest sorrow.

If our vows have not been heard, we have at least a lively hope that our prayers
may

may be useful for the repose of his soul, and procure him eternal glory.

Our hope is founded upon the love which he always professed for the Catholic Religion; his attachment to the Holy See; his good intentions towards us, of which he gave us proofs to the last moment; and lastly, upon the sincere repentance which he testified in presence of his whole Court, begging pardon of God, and his kingdom, for the errors of his life, and desiring to live only to repair them.

The same prayers which we have put up in secret for the repose of his soul, We shall put up also in public: yet That shall not hinder us from remembering him before God, to the last hour of our life.

We should declare to you, our venerable Brethren, upon this occasion, that Louis-Augustus, our most dear Son in Jesus Christ, Grandson of the late King, succeeds to the Estates and Kingdoms of his Grandfather, inheriting, at the same time, all the heroic virtues of the August House of Bourbon.

We

We already know his zeal and attachment to Religion, as well as his filial love towards us. His pathetic letters filled with affection, joined to the fame of his excellent qualities, which are every where published, are the most convincing proofs how well we have founded our expectations. We have nothing more at heart than to answer, as much as we possibly can, such laudable sentiments.

We ought at the same time to inform you, that our venerable Brother, Francis-Joachim, Cardinal of Bernis, formerly Ambassador from the late King to our Person, hath been confirmed by his credentials which he hath presented to us. In shewing you our perfect satisfaction upon that subject, we observe yours to shine forth; knowing that you are persuaded, as well as we are, that he is a most faithful interpreter both of the King's intentions and ours, in order to preserve a happy harmony.

Let us by our most ardent prayers conjure the Almighty, from whom Kings hold their crowns and kingdoms, to shed his

his most abundant blessings upon our most dear son in Jesus Christ, Louis-Augustus of France, that in the course of his reign he may enjoy all prosperity, and live in such a manner as to be useful to the cause of Religion, and advantageous to the illustrious French nation.

BULL

FOR THE

UNIVERSAL JUBILEE,

IN THE YEAR M,DCC,LXXV.

CLEMENT, Bishop, Servant of the Servants of God, to all the faithful in Jesus Christ, to whom these Letters shall come, health and Apostolical Benediction.

Jesus Christ our Lord, the Author of our Salvation, not satisfied with procuring to man, by his death and passion, a deliverance from the old slavery of sin, a return to life and liberty, an exaltation to the

the fublime title of being Co-heirs to his glory, and Children of God; has added to all thefe favours one infinitely precious, and deftined for thofe, who, having been drawn afide by human frailty, and their own perverfenefs, have unfortunately forfeited the right they had to the Divine inheritance. By the power which he gave to the Prince of Apoftles to remit fins, when he intrufted him with the keys of the kingdom of Heaven, he has procured to finners a means of expiating their fins, of recovering their firft innocence, and receiving the fruits of Redemption. As it is the only means they poffefs, who have deviated from the law of the Lord, to re-enter into friendfhip with God, and to arrive at eternal falvation, the fucceffors of St. Peter, the heirs of his power, have never had any thing more at heart than to fummon all finners to the divine fource of mercy, to offer and promife pardon to true penitents, and to invite even thofe who are held in heavy chains of fin to the hopes of a remiffion.

Although

Although, in the exercife of a duty of this importance, fo neceffary for man's falvation, it has never interrupted the cares of their Apoftolical Miniftry; they have neverthelefs judged proper to chufe and fix, in the courfe of ages, certain remarkable periods for engaging finners to foften the Divine wrath, to embrace penitence as the only plank which remains after fhipwreck; and that by the hope of a more ample harveft of graces and pardons, and by the public and general liberty to fhare the treafures of indulgence of which they are the depofitories.--And that no generation might be deprived of the precious advantages attached to thefe times of relaxation, they have fixed the return of every twenty-fifth year as the year of Jubilee, the holy year, the year of grace and remiffion, which they have ordered to be opened in the City which is looked upon as the center and feat of Religion.

We then, in conformity with fo falutary a cuftom, and one of thefe privileged years being at hand, are anxious to announce it to all of you, our dear Children, who are

united

united in the profeſſion of the ſame faith with us, and the holy Roman Catholic Church; and we exhort you to labour for the good of your ſouls, and to profit by ſuch means of ſanctification as can be the moſt effectual. We offer you a ſhare of all the riches of the Divine mercy and clemency which have been intruſted to us; and chiefly of thoſe which have their origin in the blood of Jeſus Chriſt. We will then open to you all the gates of the rich reſervoir of ſatisfactions derived from the merits of the Holy Mother of God, the holy Apoſtles, the blood of Martyrs, and the good works of all the Saints, ſo great and ſincere is our deſire to facilitate to you the recovery of peace and reconciliation.

Now, as nothing contributes more than the multitude of helps which may be expected from the communion of the Saints; united to their auguſt ſociety, we with them compoſing the body of the Church, which is one indiviſible, and that of Jeſus Chriſt himſelf, whoſe blood purifies us, enlivens us, and puts us in a condition to be uſeful to one another; to give more luſtre to the

the immensity of his love and mercy, to render more sensible the strength and infinite efficacy of his Passion, and his merits; the Redeemer of mankind hath been pleased to disperse the effects of it over all the Members of his mystick body, that they may more easily assist one another, by the communication of their reciprocal help and advantages. His intention was in this association so wisely contrived, of which his most precious blood is the beginning, and the union of hearts the whole strength, to induce the tenderness of the Eternal Father to grant his mercy to us, by presenting to Him the invaluable price of the blood of his Son, the merits of Saints, and the power of their suffrages, as the most effectual motives to determine him.

We invite you then to drink of this overflowing stream of indulgence, to enrich yourselves in the inexhaustible treasures of the Church; and, according to the custom and institution of our ancestors, the consent of our venerable Brethren the Cardinals, &c.

O all of you, then, who are the Children of the Church, do not let slip the present occasion, this favourable time, these salu-

tary days, without employing them to appease the justice of God, and obtain your pardon! Do not bring, as an excuse for your delay, the fatigues of the voyage, the troubles of the journey.---When we propose to load you with the gifts of heavenly Grace, to introduce you into the Tabernacles of the Lord, is it proper for you to let yourselves be dismayed by inconveniences, or obstacles, which never deter those whose curiosity or the thirst of gain daily lead to the most distant regions? Even those toils which might dismay you, being undertaken from so noble a motive, will assist you infinitely in reaping the most abundant fruits from your penitence. For this reason, the Church has always looked upon the old custom of Pilgrimages as singularly useful; being persuaded, that the disagreeable inconveniences which necessarily attended them, are so many compensations for past sins, and convincing proofs of sincere repentance. If the activity of your zeal, the ardour of your love for God, should kindle to such a degree as to make you forget your fatigues, or even to lessen them, be not alarmed; for that holy joy will accelerate your
recon-

reconciliation, and make a principal part of the satisfaction for thofe fins that you were charged with, *since much will be forgiven him who hath much loved.*

Haften then to the City of Sion; come and fill yourfelves with the abundance which reigns in the houfe of the Lord: Every thing here will lead you to repentance; even the afpect of this City, the ordinary habitation of Faith and Piety, the fepulchre of Apoftles, the tomb of Martyrs. When you fee this land which was fprinkled with their blood, when the numberlefs veftiges of their fanctity prefent themfelves to you on every fide, it will be impoffible for you to refift that fevere repentance which will prefs upon you, for having withdrawn from the rules and laws which they followed, and which you promifed to follow. You will find in the dignity of the Divine worfhip, in the majefty of the Temples, a powerful voice which will remind you that you are the Temple of the Living God; that he will animate you to adorn it, and with the greater zeal, for your having formerly had an inclination to profane it, and to grieve the Holy Spirit. What muft fupport your refolution, will be the groans and tears of a great number of Christians, whom you will see lamenting their errors, and soliciting their pardon with God. Very soon the sentiments of sorrow and piety, which you will witness, shall pass into your hearts with a quickness which must surprise you.

But to this holy sorrow, this religious mourning, the most tender consolations will not fail to succeed, when you see a multitude of people and nations running in crouds to practise works of justice and repentance. Can you then ever hope for a more agreeable, a more ravishing spectacle, than that of giving to the whole world a sensible image of the glorious triumph of the Cross, and of Religion? At least, on our part, we shall be happy on occasion of the almost universal re-union of the Children of the Church; persuaded that we shall find for ourselves, in the mutual efforts of your charity and piety, an ample superabundance of help and resources: for we have the fullest confidence, that when you shall have supplicated with us the Divine Distributor of Grace for the preservation of the Faith, for the return of those people who have separated from us, for the tranquility

tranquility of the Church, and the happiness of the Christian Princes, you will before your God remember your common Father, who heartily loves you; and procure, by your vows and intreaties, the strength necessary for our weakness, to support the immense load which has been imposed upon us.

And you, our venerable Brethren, Patriarchs, Primates, Archbishops and Bishops, join in our solicitude; charge yourselves with our duties and your own; declare to the people who are intrusted to you, these times of penitence and propitiation; employ all your cares, and all your authority, as much as is possible on this favourable occasion for obtaining pardon, which our paternal love has brought forth for the whole Christian world, according to the ancient practice of the Church, to produce good fruit for the salvation of souls. May they hear you explain such works of humility and Christian charity as they ought to practise, that they may be better disposed to receive the fruits of the Heavenly Grace which is offered to their wants! May they learn, both by your precepts and example, that they ought to

have

have recourse to fastings, prayer, and alms-giving.

If there be any among you, our venerable Brethren, who will take upon you, as an increase of your Pastoral labours, that of being yourselves the conductors of a part of your flock towards the City, which is the Citadel of Religion, and from whence the sources of indulgence spring, you may be assured that we will receive you with all the sensibility of the most tender father. Independent of the lustre which they will procure to our solemnity, they will be enabled, after such noble fatigues, after such meritorious labours, to reap the most ample harvest of the gifts of Divine mercy; and at their return with the rest of their flock, they will have the consolation of distributing to them this precious store.

We do not doubt that our most dear Sons, the Emperor, the Kings, and all the Christian Princes, will assist us with their authority in the vows which we make for the salvation of souls, so that they may have the happy success which we expect. We exhort them, with all our soul, to concur with us in such a manner as may correspond with their love of Religion, and the zeal of our venerable Brethren the Bishops; to favour their undertaking, and to procure safety and convenience on the roads to all Pilgrims. They cannot but know, that such cares must contribute greatly to the tranquility of their reign; and that God will be the more propitious and favourable to them, the more they shew themselves attentive to increase his glory for the good of the People.

But in the end, that these Presents may come, &c.

> Given at ROME, at St. MARIE-MAJOR, &c. in the Year of our LORD, 1774. the 12th of May, and the 5th Year of our Pontificate.

THIS Bull, with which I finish this collection, may be looked upon as the Testament of Clement XIV. Death, which from that time was ready to seize him, gave him an inward warning that his end was approaching, that he might speak to the Faithful for the last time, and that God required the sacrifice of his life.

Every one shared in the misfortune; and all Communions, however differing in their persuasions, united in praying to the Lord for the preservation of a Pontiff, who was so agreeable to all the crowned heads, and beloved by the whole world. Some recollected the goodness with which he had received them; others, his love of wisdom and peace; while he himself, regardless of the severe ills which he endured, employed his interrupted respiration in sighing to Heaven for the obtaining the kingdom of truth and concord upon Earth, and to leave after him some vestiges of his love for peace and justice.

I was desirous to procure some of the Letters he wrote during the six last months of his life, which was a time of trial and pain, but could not possibly obtain them. However, we have enough to shew us, that this great Pontiff adhered essentially to the fundamentals of Religion, without being attached to any opinion, and without having the least spirit of Party. What is certain, is, that nothing but Prejudice can with-hold his praise;—Posterity must value him according to his merit, and sincerely lament their not having known him. Neither passion, cabals nor prejudice, will be capable of obscuring his glory—and Truth alone will present his picture.

www.ingramcontent.com/pod-product-compliance
Lightning Source LLC
Chambersburg PA
CBHW031944230426
43672CB00010B/2041